MW01640972

TABLE

INTRODUCTION

King Solomon, wrote the proverbs as a father to his son—wisdom for a future dad. So also, these ten-minute devotions from Proverbs are a gift to new dads who have taken up the blessed privilege of fatherhood. I have written primarily to Christian dads, though all are invited to peer into this window of biblical parenting.

Our family is by no means a model of perfection, but fellow travelers following the path of God's wisdom with every bend in the road presenting still further challenges. By God's grace, I am repeatedly humbled as I learn through both successes and failures how to raise my children as my heavenly Father is raising me. Only by God's all-sufficient Word "the man of God may be competent, equipped for every good work" (2 Tim. 3:17). I hope you will read these verses from God's Word, consider the practical wisdom they offer, and be drawn in by the beauty of God's design for your family.

Each devotion begins with a Proverb to be written down and memorized. I encourage you to reflect on it throughout the day and treasure it in your heart. You will be blessed by the overflowing benefits of God's enduring wisdom. I also share humorous anecdotes from our own family's experience to demonstrate how the wisdom of Proverbs applies to everyday life. Each devotion includes an explanation from Scripture and ends with a simple prayer to direct your heart to God. Consider writing your prayer of response or ideas for application in the space provided. May you be blessed by the reading and application of God's Word!

—1—

THE FEAR OF THE LORD

The fear of the LORD is the beginning of wisdom,
and the knowledge of the Holy One is insight.

PROVERBS 9:10

My three boys learned many of the proverbs on our ten-minute drive to school. For example, I would call out, "Proverbs 1:7. The fear of the Lord is the beginning of wisdom," and they would repeat: "Proverbs 1:7. The fear of the Lord is the beginning of wisdom."

Then I would say, "Fools despise wisdom and instruction," and they would echo, "Fools despise wisdom and instruction."

We would do this multiple times until they could cite the verse from memory. And if one of them learned it before the others, he would then teach his brothers until they could all recite it in unison.

After memorizing each verse, we would discuss it together: "*What does it mean to fear the Lord*?" "To love him and obey him because of who he is."

"*So why is the fear of the Lord the beginning of knowledge*?" "Because if we love God and obey his Word, we will grow in knowledge about the world God has made."

"*What does it mean to despise*?" "It means to hate—to refuse to listen."

"*But why does the fool despise wisdom and instruction*?" "Because he doesn't know what's good for him."

The Proverbs became a catechism encouraging our children to meditate on God's Word. We trained them to store up God's Word in their hearts as an investment for future withdrawals.

For example, a few days later, one boy expressed his terror over a scary, spiral staircase, which led to our backyard. So I said to him, "I know it feels scary, but you don't need to be afraid. You can trust me." We discussed the difference between healthy and unhealthy kinds of fear. Then I said to him, "Remember Proverbs 1:7?" Once he recited it, I explained, "If you fear the

Lord, you will not have unhealthy fears. You can trust the Lord and you can trust daddy as the one God gave to protect you."

He replied, "I'm still afraid, but I will go up-and-down the scary stairs." And he did it! His legs were trembling, but he did it! Then he did it again and again! His brothers were cheering and he was exuberant. That night during our family worship he prayed without any prompting: "Thank you, Jesus, for helping me go up-and-down the scary stairs."

Now I am certain my boys will face greater dangers in life than scary stairs, but I want them to store up God's Word in their hearts for those crucial moments of faith. Dads, remind your children (and yourself) that depositing God's Word in your spiritual bank will pay abundant dividends in the long-run.

The fear of the Lord comprises two complementary aspects: reverent obedience and worshipful joy. Imagine you are the crown prince of a royal kingdom. Any citizen, including the prince, may be lawfully executed for crimes of treason, so your fear of the king keeps you from rebellion. Yet the king is also your father to whom you run for loving embrace. In that embrace, your fear of the king—your knowledge of his power and sovereignty, his might and justice also serves as your protection. You feel absolutely safe in the arms of the most powerful person in the land.

So also, the fear of the Lord becomes your security as you rest on his unchanging attributes. Although you are commanded to obey him, it is also your desire. You are motivated both by the joy of his presence and the fear of his displeasure. You tremble at his justice should you break his commands, yet rejoice in praise because "the fear of the LORD is a fountain of life" (Prov. 14:27). The fear of the Lord is both reverent obedience and worshipful joy.

Dads, as you study Proverbs, realize that God has given you sufficient strength and wisdom for each day. He shows you what will happen if you follow his Word and what will happen if you don't. So if you desire to raise God-fearing children, then you must first fear the Lord yourself.

PRAYER: *Dear Heavenly Father, Show me how to both revere your holiness and delight in your love. Teach me how to be a good father by trusting in you as my heavenly Father. Equip me to raise God-fearing children who love you and worship you as well. In your Son's name, Amen.*

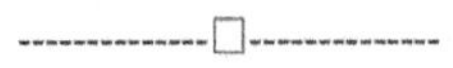

Write down one way you will apply today's Proverb:

—————2—————

WISDOM & INSTRUCTION

The fear of the LORD is instruction in wisdom,
and humility comes before honor.
- PROVERBS 15:33

As a concerned father, it always frightened me when my boys ran out into the street as they often did. So I never brushed it off with a wave of my hand: "Ahhh, boys will be boys." I did not compliment their speed and agility or wait for something terrible to happen, hoping they would learn from their mistakes. (There is a time and place for that, but not in the middle of the street). Instead, I would shout with urgency, "Stop! Get out of the street!" I reprimanded out of love because my rules were for their good, just as God's rules are for our good. In the safety of our home, I then carefully explained why I did not want them running in the street.

The diligent student of Proverbs will first seek "to know wisdom" (1:2a). The verb "to know" implies intimate relationship, for the prudent father understands how wisdom relates to everyday life. Such wisdom for living must come from God because worldly expertise can hardly navigate the storms of life. Thus Solomon has arranged the Proverbs under the fear of the LORD (1:7; 9:10; 31:30) and places every element of wisdom within this framework: How does the God-ness of God—his attributes and actions affect your relationships and desires, your finances and parenting, your fears and struggles? The Proverbs are decidedly God-centered, for mere human knowledge is not enough to meet life's problems. Therefore, the wisdom to handle life with God-honoring skill asks the question: "Do my decisions draw me closer to the Lord or drive me further away?"

Secondly, dads, Solomon also desires that you experientially know the "instruction" of God (1:2a), which involves correction for the sake of direction. The proverbs disrupt your life in order to instruct and tear you up in order to piece you back together. As imperfect people born in sin, we all need loving instruction from our heavenly Father. Picture the day when your child first learns to walk. You are delighted by those faltering steps and cheer as she toddles forward. You rejoice not because you envision a day he will walk away from you, but because you dream for the day he will walk along beside you. In like manner, you must raise your children spiritually "in the discipline and instruction of the Lord" (Eph. 6:4b), so that they might one day walk beside you as brothers and sisters in Christ. Godly instruction develops godly character.

Dads, make your instruction directive in nature and detailed in content, for young children must be taught to obey step-by-step. They do not have the maturity to know what to do unless you instruct them patiently. Sometimes I would drop off my boys at school and toss them some generic instructions like, "Be good. Have fun." Then at other times I would hold their face in my hands: "Make sure you look your teacher in the eye and say, 'Good morning, teacher.' Don't just stand there and say nothing." Specific instruction lets my children know what I expect of them, then brings conviction if they do not obey. So also, the book of Proverbs is a road map for life: "Go here and not there. Turn right and not left. Avoid that street. Beware of danger." There is a definite path to a secure destination. You might be able to choose your actions, but you cannot choose the consequences (see Prov. 4:25-27).

Finally dads, realize that only God can change your child's heart in order for instruction to take root: "The fear of the LORD is instruction in wisdom, and humility comes before honor" (15:33). You are responsible to teach God's wisdom, yet your child must be willing to accept it. Just as one player passes the ball to another, so also "a wise son hears his father's instruction" (13:1a) and "whoever loves discipline loves knowledge" (12:1a). Children must apply the wisdom they learn because the benefits of discipline are not automatically enjoyed. The proverbs are not helpful if we read, but do not heed. What then, dads, is your responsibility to teach God's wisdom as a parent, a teacher, a discipler, or a counselor? What is your responsibility to learn and apply God's Word yourself?

Envision a father and son walking hand-in-hand as they converse about life. Solomon recalls his own father, David: "He taught me and said to me, 'Let your heart hold fast my words; keep my commandments, and live'" (4:4). These "commandments" (the *torah*) catechize a specific body of truth recorded in the Proverbs and recited by Israel. The appeal to grandpa David reveals that these teachings have stood the test of time. Thus Solomon exhorts his son to remember them in his heart until they are obeyed and not merely heard.

PRAYER: *Dear Heavenly Father, Teach me to know wisdom and instruction. Shine your light on my study of Proverbs to help me learn and apply its truths. Instruct me in the biblical path of fatherhood, so I can instruct my children accordingly. Help me to know you more and more each day through the study of your Word. In your Son's name, Amen.*

-------------□-------------

Write down one way you will apply today's Proverb:

3

DISCERNMENT

Trust in the LORD with all your heart,
and do not lean on your own understanding.
In all your ways acknowledge him,
and he will make straight your paths.
- PROVERBS 3:5-6

One challenge of raising boys is that they are perpetually hungry (except at mealtimes when they like to mess around). I must often remind my boys, "No, you may not have a snack half-an-hour before dinner," "Sugar is not a food group," and, "Yes, you do have to eat your vegetables."

Dads, when your children are young, you will make most of their decisions for them. Yet as they grow older, you teach them to take responsibility: "What do you think about your friend's comment? What's the right decision in this situation? What are some ways you can spend your birthday money? What makes this college better than that one?" You train your children how to make decisions on their own, so that when they leave your home they possess a measure of wisdom for themselves.

Suppose my son goes off to college and one day gives me a call: "Hey dad. The guys are going out for pizza Friday night. Can I go? Can I?"

I would say to him, "Son, that's on you. I have trained you to make wise choices and I'm always here if you need to talk, but I will not make your every decision." We all know there's something wrong if we treat our children the same at eighteen years as we did at eighteen months.

The student of Proverbs must "understand words of insight" (Prov. 1:2b). The root word, "to understand" (repeated twice in the Hebrew for emphasis) means to divide in two and thus to separate. As Solomon had prayed, "Give your servant therefore an understanding mind to govern your people, that I may discern between good and evil, for who is able to govern this your great people?" (1 Kgs. 3:9). Discernment is being able to separate right from wrong, good from evil, truth from lies, and temporal pleasures from eternal values. It is the ability to look at two options and see what God sees. Thus right discernment must be based upon the Word of God. According to Proverbs 3:5, "Trust in the LORD with all your heart, and do not lean on your own [discernment]."

Dads, many situations, which seem hazy at first, will become more and more clear as you seek God's counsel in his Word. You will not see what God sees until you know what he has given you to know. So ask yourself: "This past week, what was the hardest decision you had to make? How did you know the right thing to do and did you finally make the right decision?" Discernment is looking at two options and seeing the truth which God sees.

The Bible, however, is not a topical index providing answers for every life decision. Rather, God's Word guides you into a conversation with your Creator. Proverbs has much to say about choosing the right path, acting in wisdom, receiving blessed rewards, and avoiding deadly consequences. Yet the fear of the Lord underlies everything as the foundation of wisdom (1:7). God's primary purpose in decision-making is not that you make all the right choices, but that you mature as you grow in relationship with him. So try not to focus on individual decisions: "What school? Which job? Whom to marry? Where to live?" Instead, ask yourself at the end of each decision: "Have I grown in reverent obedience and worshipful joy in the Lord my God?" The truth God desires you to see is ultimately himself.

PRAYER: *Dear Heavenly Father, Enable me to see the truth in your Word and grant me discernment in the decisions of life. Like Solomon becoming king, I feel young and inexperienced as a new dad. Give your servant therefore an understanding mind to father my children that I may discern between good and evil. For who is able to undertake this daunting task alone? Help me to trust in you with all my heart, instead of leaning on my own understanding. In your Son's name, Amen.*

--------------□--------------

Write down one way you will apply today's Proverb:

4

RIGHTEOUSNESS, JUSTICE AND EQUITY

To receive instruction in wise dealing,
in righteousness, justice, and equity.
- PROVERBS 1:3

The other day, one of my boys struck his brother with malicious intent because he wanted the toy that his brother was not sharing. He then spit out the most horrible insult he could conjure: "You're not my best friend." His sense of fairness had been violated, so he sought to make things right by force. Realize dads, that you are often called upon as judge and jury because your children are infinitely creative in finding ways to fight. Study Proverbs, therefore, "to receive instruction in wise dealing, in righteousness, justice, and equity" (1:3). "To receive instruction" again restates the need for "discipline" (v. 2a) and "wise dealing" describes the discernment and insight to reason your way through complex situations. Discernment is knowing what God wants, whereas insight is knowing why he wants it.

"Wise dealing" then trickles down to the ethical results of "righteousness, justice, and equity." Who you are determines how you act as character leads to conduct and then to consequences. The wise in Proverbs are righteous and the righteous wise since God's perfect will is always the wisest course of action. Our world mistakenly believes that children are inherently good and will eventually meander in the right decision. A child's heart problem, however, is not ignorance, but lack of wisdom rooted in a sinful nature (22:15a). So dads, do not appeal to the wisdom of your child's internal goodness but to the external Word of God. God's Word alone reveals the right way to live in the world which God created and still sustains. God's way produces a righteousness unheard of by the world.

Consider also "justice." Does your child live in accord with both the rules of the man and the rules of God? Learn from Proverbs how to speak with your child about injustice. Look for ways to help the underprivileged and serve with ministries seeking to right the wrongs in this fallen world. Then relate everything back to Scripture by discussing accounts of God's justice with your child.

"Equity" comes from the meaning of being "level" or "even." The wise speak uprightly without placing hindrances in the path of others: "Hear, for I will speak noble things, and from my lips will come what is right" (8:6b). When your child complains, "It's not fair," then take the opportunity to gently instruct her about the meaning of equity. Show her how thankful we should be that God gave us mercy and grace instead of what was fair (Rom. 6:23).

Finally dads, consider your example: Are you righteous before God and righteous before others? Are you humble in your personal walk (Mic. 6:8)? Such righteousness, justice, and equity require wisdom. Thus James invites you to request: "If any of you lacks wisdom, let him ask God, who gives generously to all without reproach, and it will be given him" (Jas. 1:5). Specifically ask for divine wisdom which can be found in no other source. Ask with passion, not passivity (vv. 6-8), for the Proverbs describe godly wisdom as elusive, hard-fought, and difficult to obtain. The Proverbs require much effort to understand and apply. Therefore, you must cry out with the psalmist: "Open my eyes, that I may behold wondrous things out of your law. . . . Incline my heart to your testimonies, and not to selfish gain!" (Ps. 119:18, 36). God will generously grant wisdom when you pray, yet he speaks that wisdom through the study of his Word. You cannot lounge around like spiritual royalty as servants stuff grapes of wisdom into your mouth. Instead, labor in the vineyard of Proverbs, plucking each juicy grape like succulent fruit from the vine. Savor each truth until the juice seeps into your soul.

Dads, have you diligently asked the Lord for the wisdom to live rightly? If not, write down a few areas of life where you desperately need the wisdom of God. Pray for wisdom in these areas, then wait actively on the Lord. Open up the book of Proverbs, for God grants wisdom to those who seek it.

PRAYER: *Dear Heavenly Father, Instruct me in wise dealings at work, at home, in my relationships, and with my finances. Teach me to walk every day in righteousness, justice, and equity. Show me how I can be godly even in a* *fallen world that is not always fair. In your Son's name, Amen.*

--------------□--------------

Write down one way you will apply today's Proverb:

———————5———————

PRUDENCE, KNOWLEDGE, AND DISCRETION

To give prudence to the simple,
knowledge and discretion to the youth.
- PROVERBS 1:4

Like many parents, I cannot count the times I've shouted after my retreating boys, "Shut the door!" Always in a hurry to reach their destination, they neglect to finish the task behind them. Certainly their folly is a symptom of forgetfulness, but an even greater folly concerns me as their father. I must teach them to shut the door of their mind after truth has entered in. Thus Proverbs 1:4 introduces still more blessings in God's Word: "To give prudence to the simple, knowledge and discretion to the youth." This verse describes two types of people who most need wisdom: the simple and the young. And dads, realize that your children are both.

The gullible minds of the "simple" are a literal open space to be crammed with anything and everything (see 14:15a). Being "open-minded" may sound virtuous to a pluralistic society, yet Scripture describes it as a dangerous condition. Picture a house with the front door swinging wide open. Any manner of pest might fly through the gaping doorway, while trespassers can enter unhindered. So also, the open-minded child lets in evil thoughts without discernment and allows good thoughts to escape without retention. He is untrained, inexperienced, and unprincipled in his ways. For the mind of the simple is open on both ends, creating a wind tunnel between the ears.

The second category of "youth" could refer to any age from infancy to young adulthood, but Proverbs mainly presents him as one who lacks maturity (see 7:7; 20:11; 22:6, 15; 23:13). I once caught my boys trying to down a whole jar of gummy vitamins because they thought it would help them grow faster. I had to explain how growth takes time, both physically and spiritually. Wisdom is necessary for both the simple and the youth—the naïve and the immature. Solomon presents the remedy for both.

The simple need "prudence," an old-fashioned term meaning to be "clever" or "crafty" with godly shrewdness and spiritual insight. As Jesus told his disciples, "Be wise as serpents and innocent as doves" (Matt. 10:16b). So "in everything the prudent acts with knowledge, but a fool flaunts his folly" (Prov. 13:16). Prudence is a Spirit-born cleverness to see the trends and dangers of life before they arrive. For example, Joseph foresaw the danger of adultery with Potiphar's wife (e.g., Gen. 39) and again displayed shrewdness in preparing Egypt for the famine (e.g., Gen. 41). The simple need prudence to know when to open and close the gates of the mind.

Youth must learn "knowledge" both personally and experientially. Here lies the difference between medical school and residency; the bar exam and the courtroom; seminary and the pastorate. Dads, let your children observe God's wisdom in your everyday life as they apply it to theirs. Study the Proverbs so you can discuss wisdom at the dinner table as you address particular problems your family is facing. Children acquire knowledge both through observation and practice.

In addition, youth must learn "discretion": the ability to plan wisely and to avoid dangerous folly. According to Proverbs 2:11, "Discretion will watch over you, understanding will guard you." Youth need the protection of Proverbs, for they live in a fallen world where foolish decisions lead to disaster. So dads, are your children gullible and immature? Are they young and naïve? Then study the Proverbs to teach them prudence, knowledge, and discretion.

PRAYER: *Dear Heavenly Father, I am simple in my understanding of your Word and still a youth when it comes to wisdom. Teach me prudence, knowledge, and discretion as I grow in my faith as a father. Then show me* *how to pass on these truths to my children, so I might spare them future harm. In your Son's name, Amen.*

--------------□--------------

Write down one way you will apply today's Proverb:

6

GUIDANCE

Let the wise hear and increase in learning,
and the one who understands obtain guidance.
- PROVERBS 1:5

Many fathers enjoy playing ball with their sons and our house is no exception. We often play catch in the yard, basketball in the driveway, football on any empty stretch of floor, and (much to my wife's consternation) broom hockey in the front entryway. Yet even as we play for fun, the coach in me sometimes calls, "Timeout," to offer guidance: "Catch the ball with two hands. Follow through on your passes. That's a double-dribble." Guidance requires the recognition of wrong behavior and the wisdom to correct it.

"Let the wise hear and increase in learning," writes Solomon, "and the one who understands obtain guidance" (Prov. 1:5). "The one who understands" is the man of discernment (v. 2b) who must "obtain" or purchase "guidance" at a price (see 4:5, 7). It takes substantial effort to make wisdom one's own. Consider a possession you really desire. You think about it and dream about it. You work, scrounge, and comparison-shop. Then you travel to the store and purchase that item to claim it as yours. Such is the effort we must make to obtain wisdom. Yet if someone watched a video of your life this past week, would it be clear that you were intentionally pursuing wisdom? Were your thoughts, desires, and actions all focused on obtaining guidance from the Lord?

"Guidance" originally referred to the ropes that sailors would pull to steer the rudder or turn the sails of a ship, thus the nautical phrase "knowing the ropes." So dads, you must guide your children to navigate their way through complex problems—to see the end from the beginning and to know each successive step which must be taken.

Some truths, of course, are easier to teach: "Look both ways before crossing the street. Work hard; play hard. Pay off your credit cards. Choose a spouse carefully." Yet wisdom knows the right choice to make when the rules aren't black-and-white. You cannot prepare your child for every situation, so you must teach him how to wisely apply biblical principles. Dads, do your children know the ropes of life? Can they discern what will likely happen should they make this decision or that one?

Your child needs your loving guidance because he lives in a fallen world. As Solomon warns against the enticement of sinners:

> My son, do not walk in the way with them; hold back your foot from their paths, for their feet run to evil, and they make haste to shed blood. For in vain is a net spread in the sight of any bird, but these men lie in wait for their own blood; they set an ambush for their own lives. Such are the ways of everyone who is greedy for unjust gain; it takes away the life of its possessors (1:15-19).

One time as birds were visiting our backyard, my boys chattered excitedly about putting out a cage to catch them (as if some bird would hop into their cage and close the door on itself). Solomon tells us, "No bird is that dumb. They laugh at the fool who spreads out a net in plain sight or who sprinkles seed to set a trap." The wicked, however, are dumber than the birds and foolishly ensnared by their own net. They "lie in wait for blood" (v. 11) until that blood becomes their own. They "ambush the innocent" (v. 18), yet are ambushed themselves in a mutual bloodbath. "Such are the ways of everyone who is greedy for unjust gain; it takes away the life of its possessors" (v. 19). They themselves are the ones swallowed up by death in the pit of Sheol (v. 12). Thus Solomon warns his son: "Don't even go down that path or experiment with sin. Take a lesson from the birds and fly from evil. The wise man avoids trouble by refusing to associate with the wicked." Dads, your guidance helps your child spot the fools by using the Proverbs as a training manual for godly living. May "the one who understands obtain guidance."

PRAYER: *Dear Heavenly Father, I need guidance from your Word to properly lead my children away from danger and into your presence. Teach me to be a wise and loving spiritual coach in their lives. Help me to see where they need to grow and how to guide them in the right path. In your Son's name, Amen.*

--------------□--------------

Write down one way you will apply today's Proverb:

—7—

HEART DESIRES

Keep your heart with all vigilance,
for from it flow the springs of life.
- PROVERBS 4:23

Dads, have you ever noticed what upsets you? Your wife asks you to take out the trash and you get angry. You gripe and complain, then afterwards think: "Where did that come from?" Or you're in the fast lane, content to drive the speed limit and some car tries to pass you on the right. So you hit the gas (because now it's a race that you must win). Your accelerating opponent has the element of surprise, however, and cuts you off. As you slam on the brakes, you curse him out (under your breath, of course, because you're a Christian). Dads, why do you yell at your kids for being late? Or why does your toddler smack his brother in the head with a fire truck? Why does your teenager stomp off to her room and slam the door? "What causes quarrels and what causes fights among you? Is it not this, that your passions are at war within you? You desire and do not have, so you murder. You covet and cannot obtain, so you fight and quarrel" (Jas. 4:1-2). What are you getting that you're not wanting? What are you wanting that you're not getting?

One night, I was exhausted from fighting an illness and fretting about everything I had to do in the coming week, when my wife asked me for a simple favor that would have required five minutes of minimal effort. She asked very sweetly without a guilt trip, accusation, or ultimatum. Sadly, my first response was to grumble with anger. As I was later convicted by my failure, I realized the desire of my heart was comfort. I wanted rest—a good desire, which I had foolishly made into an idolatrous, inordinate demand. I was not getting the relaxation I wanted. Even though I loved my wife and desired to serve her, my passions and desires were at war within me. In that moment, I was not serving my wife or honoring the Lord but rather choosing to please myself. Now my response had taken place in a split second, but I had spent the entire day dwelling on that idol of comfort. The boiling point of my anger revealed my heart's desire like warning sirens at a nuclear power plant. So dads, when you get angry, pay attention! God is about to expose the idols which you value more than him.

So also, you must address your child's sinful heart. Look at your child and just add ten years. If he continues down his current path, where will he end up ten years from now? Is he headed toward eternal life or eternal death? Does he need your help to adjust his course? One day, you will no longer be able to instruct him. He will be out of your house, semi-independent, making decisions on his own (most of which you'll know nothing about). Are you preparing him for that day? Like Solomon, you must call him to pay attention: "My son, be attentive to my words; incline your ear to my sayings. Let them not escape from your sight; keep them within your heart" (Prov. 4:20-21). Solomon even wrote out his instruction for clarity: "Let my sayings and proverbs not escape from your sight. I have written them down for you. Read them often. Keep them always before your eyes. Most importantly, keep them within your heart. Guard them. Protect them. Memorize them. Meditate on them. Let my words remain fixed in your heart and settled in your soul."

Using the anatomy of discipleship, Solomon speaks of eyes and ears (vv. 20-21, 25), of life and flesh (v. 22). He shapes the mouth with speech and talk (v. 24) and highlights the path with feet that walk (vv. 26-27). Yet the center of this passage describes the heart as the control center of the body and the mind: "Keep your heart with all vigilance, for from it flow the springs of life" (v. 23). The heart is the inner man—the soul—the personality—the seat of thoughts, emotions, and desires. The heart tells you what we want, then directs your body (which includes the brain) to carry out its wishes. Therefore, the desire to gain wisdom and the decision to choose the righteous path both begin in the heart.

Guard your heart to control your body and its fleshly desires (1 John 2:16). Solomon pictures a prison guard standing at attention or a sentry keeping watch over city walls. Guard your heart, for every word you speak, every act of behavior, and every sinful response to suffering comes straight out of the heart (Luke 6:43-45). Even if sinful words and actions appear involuntary, you have likely been pouring junk into your heart for years.

Guard your heart, "for from it flow the springs of life." If water from your well poisons a friend, don't blame your friend for drinking the water. Check the source. So also, if you explode in anger at a loved one or find yourself paralyzed by unexplainable fears, then perhaps your heart has been polluted (Mark 7:15, 21-23). You do what you do because you want what you want. Guard your heart and you will not only resist temptation, but also bear good fruit (Gal. 5:22-23).

PRAYER: *Dear Heavenly Father, Help me to guard my heart from sin and temptation. Teach me to walk your path of wisdom and bear good fruit. I cannot do this on my own, but only by your grace and power. Help me to guard my heart and to teach my children how to guard theirs. In your Son's name, Amen.*

---------------□-------------

Write down one way you will apply today's Proverb:

8

AUTHORITY

Better is open rebuke than hidden love.
Faithful are the wounds of a friend;
profuse are the kisses of an enemy.
- PROVERBS 27:5-6

Dads, let your words reflect God's holy Word, so you can say to your children: "Keep my instruction" in the same breath as you say, "Receive God's wisdom." Teach them that if they please the Lord, then they also please you. You speak for God, not yourself, and especially not for them. Your children, however, will often test your parental authority with the penetrating question: "*Why?*"

"Go wash your hands before supper, dear." "*Why?*"

"It's time for bed." "*Why?*"

"Clean up your room, please." "*Why?*"

Certainly as parents we encourage curiosity. We want our children asking "Why?" of the world. Yet their knee-jerk response of asking, "Why?" is too often just a clever attempt to disobey. They are not asking why soap and water cleanses the microbes from their fingers or why a clean room is preferred to a messy one. They are questioning our God-ordained authority and asking why we have the right to interrupt their playtime. Sadly, the standard parental response (as if from a manual) is, "Because I told you so."

I had such an opportunity when one of my boys said, "I'm thirsty."

So I replied, "Okay, go get your milk."

He snapped at me with attitude, "No! I'm not going to get my milk!"

You could hear the collective gasp around the dinner table: "Oh no, he didn't!" I think he even surprised himself. I knew I had to say something quickly as I felt the eyeballs of my other boys boring into the back of my head. So after picking up my jaw from off the ground, I said to him very calmly: "Who's the daddy? Who's the son? Who listens to whom?" My son then immediately went to get his milk. Why? Because I told him so.

Scripture, however, provides us with an even better response: "I told you because God told me. God has appointed me in his Word to be your earthly authority who will teach you the wisdom of God for your protection and your benefit. God has also appointed you by his sovereignty to be my child and to trust me as your God-given authority (see Eph. 6:1)." Many children think they have it all figured out and are ready to take charge of their life, yet God has given them parents for their own protection and guidance. He commands children: "'Honor your father and mother' (this is the first commandment with a promise), 'that it may go well with you and that you may live long in the land'" (vv. 2-3). Parents possess wisdom to keep children safe, both physically and spiritually, from the dangers of this world. They might be wrong at times or occasionally provoke their children to anger (v. 4a), but children are still commanded to obey their parents in the Lord (v. 1).

The pattern of wisdom teaching in Proverbs describes fathers instructing their sons who then become fathers who instruct their own sons. It's not the other way around. Parents do not go to children for advice, but to someone wiser, and ultimately to the eternal God for biblical counsel. Dads, you don't ask your children for advice about marriage or taxes or real estate. So why should you let them run the home? Instead, may wisdom cascade down the generations like a fountain of life (13:14). Instruct your children, "I told you because God told me."

PRAYER: *Dear Heavenly Father, Help me to parent my children under your authority and remind me that my authority is God-given and directed for my children's good. Teach me to be tender toward my children both through my words and loving care. Guide me to only say to them what you have said to me in your Word. In your Son's name, Amen.*

--------------□--------------

Write down one way you will apply today's Proverb:

9

PROTECTION

Get wisdom; get insight; do not forget,
and do not turn away from the words of my mouth.
Do not forsake her, and she will keep you;
love her, and she will guard you.

- PROVERBS 4:5-6

Our family recently welcomed a baby girl into the world. After three boys, God finally gave us a girl. And as her father, the experience is vastly different. My little girl may look the same as her brothers at that age (apart from the fancy pink clothes). She poops and pees the same and squawks and waves her arms around. She sleeps the same as they did. Yet I personally experience a different feeling when I hold her. It finally struck me one day that the difference was not in her, but me. I felt more tenderness for my baby girl and a greater desire to protect her. I worried about her more than I worried about my boys. Whether because she was a helpless infant or my first little girl, I was more concerned for her protection.

Dads, you have a God-given desire to protect your children from harmful people, foolish decisions, and various hardships. You cannot protect them from every danger, but you must provide the opportunity to flourish. Realize also that God has appointed you to protect them spiritually by teaching them God's Word. Therefore, Solomon expresses to his son the importance of finding wisdom like he would find a good wife: "Get wisdom; get insight; do not forget, and do not turn away from the words of my mouth" (Prov. 4:5; see v. 7). He exhorts his son to acquire wisdom, for wisdom is like a bride who requires a dowry for her hand in marriage: "Use up all your time, your energy, and resources to acquire this pearl of great price. Though she may cost you everything, do all it takes to make her your wife. Do not forsake her, and she will keep you" (see v. 6a). As written in many Bibles, "Your sin will keep you from this Book or this Book will keep you from your sin." God's wisdom protects you from playing the fool: "Love her, and she will guard you. . . . Prize her highly, and she will exalt you; she will honor you if you embrace her" (vv. 6b, 8). Lift up Lady Wisdom and she will lift you up as well. Esteem her as your wife and know her intimately. Do not simply purchase her for a price, but also cherish her in your tender embrace. Then "she will place on your head a graceful garland; she will bestow on you a beautiful crown" (v. 9). She will bring you honor, for "an excellent wife is the crown of her husband" (12:4a).

Solomon instructs, "My son, do not lose sight of these—keep sound wisdom and discretion, and they will be life for your soul and adornment for your neck" (3:21-22; see 1:9; 3:3). "Then you will walk on your way securely, and your foot will not stumble. If you lie down, you will not be afraid; when you lie down, your sleep will be sweet" (3:23-24; see Ps. 91:12). Every dad wants his children to be safe: "Don't run with scissors. Don't eat the glue. Not too close to the edge. Beware of stranger danger. Look both ways before you cross the street." Yet how many dads instruct their children: "Know God's Word down to your inmost parts. Keep sound wisdom and discretion, and they will be life for your soul and adornment for your neck." Wisdom shows what path to take, where to place each step, and how to sleep without anxiety.

I learned this personally while spending a few days in the hospital as my son recovered from a dangerously high fever. We did get to ride in an ambulance (sirens blaring), but it was heartrending as a father to watch my son get poked and prodded and hooked up to all kinds of tubes and machines. As I waited by his crib, I meditated on Daniel 2 where Nebuchadnezzar, the king of Babylon, has just threatened to execute Daniel and his three friends and all the other wise men unless they could interpret the dream he had the night before: "Read my mind and tell me God's message or I will kill you!" Such a demand would stress out anyone, but not Daniel who remained supernaturally composed as he cast his cares upon the faithful, sovereign God. In that hospital room, I read, "Then Daniel went to his house and made the matter known to Hananiah, Mishael, and Azariah, his companions, and told them to seek mercy from the God of heaven concerning this mystery" (Dan. 2:17). Although Daniel was about to get all of his body parts chopped into pieces, he called a prayer meeting. Then he told his friends, "Do not pray for mercy from the king of Babylon. Instead, pray for mercy from the King of Heaven." God graciously reminded me through his Word: "I am the God in heaven who loves your child even more than you. I am the God in heaven who has a better plan for your life than you." Dads, you must protect your children, but also trust that God in heaven is protecting you.

PRAYER: *Dear Heavenly Father, I worry knowing that I cannot protect my children from everything. Teach me to guard them from danger, but to ultimately entrust them to you. Empower me to guide them in your wisdom so that they are blessed as they seek your will. Grant them mercy and grace by your sovereign hand. In your Son's name, Amen.*

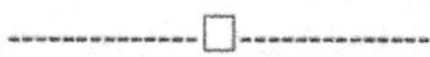

Write down one way you will apply today's Proverb:

—10—

PLANTING SEEDS

I have taught you the way of wisdom;
I have led you in the paths of uprightness.
When you walk, your step will not be hampered,
and if you run, you will not stumble.
- PROVERBS 4:11-12

My wife once planted a vegetable garden and, every day, she would water her tomatoes, pull out weeds, and watch for predatory worms and snails. She trained her tomatoes to climb a trellis and tenderly drew them back if they were turning one way or the other. So also, parenting is an everyday process. One of our sons went through a phase requiring discipline multiple times a day (often for the same offense), it was exhausting to deal with the tantrums, deception, and defiance. But one day at the breakfast table, my boys commented that I hadn't had to discipline them all year long. Their claim was not entirely accurate, but the moments had thankfully grown fewer and farther between. Dads, just like tomatoes, you cannot expect your children to grow up straight without your help. Leave them alone and they will surely bear weeds. Terrible twos become terrible teens, then terrible twenties and thirties and forties. Their hearts must be cultivated to grow in godliness, so wisely tend your garden to spare your children from folly.

First, start training them when they are young. As Solomon affectionately states, "When I was a son with my father, tender, the only one in the sight of my mother" (Prov. 4:3). He recalls his own childhood when he was still a tender shoot, capable of training. The word "tender" meant to be "gentle" or "soft," for this young prince was yet unformed both in body and soul—undeveloped and naïve in his formative years. Dads, start training your children now while they are young and tender, for it is easier to train a sapling than an oak.

Second, realize that the full benefits of raising children will not be seen immediately. Like the old Chinese proverb: "One generation plants the trees; the next generation enjoys the shade." Spiritual wisdom involves planting seeds in the soil of your children's lives, so that God's blessings will be multiplied for future generations. The other day, my boys were eating cherries and uncharacteristically sucking every vestige of fruit from off the seed. Yet instead of throwing them in the trash, they informed me with pride: "We're going to plant cherry seeds somewhere in the backyard. Then we can have cherries whenever we want." I didn't bother to ask where they were planting the seeds, whether they had tilled the soil, or if they intended to water their garden every day. I just figured it would keep them busy for at least an hour. It seems that every child has had such fantasies of growing outrageously fertile crops with relatively no effort at all. Just throw some seeds over your shoulder and they will magically sprout into trees.

Jesus, however, made quite a different claim: "Truly, truly, I say to you, unless a grain of wheat falls into the earth and dies, it remains alone; but if it dies, it bears much fruit" (John 12:24). Jesus was not describing a magic bean or a wishful grain of wheat, but using a metaphor well-known in his agrarian society. Every farmer knew that if you planted a seed in the ground—if you watered it and waited—if God blessed the crop with sufficient rain and sunlight, then at the harvest that tiny seed of grain would bear much fruit. Jesus made the point that in order for new life to grow, that seed of grain must die. It must be planted in the ground—in the darkness devoid of sunlight. It must decompose until its hardened husk is cracked, giving way to the new life which grows within. Only then does the seed bear fruit.

Likewise, dads, parenting is a grace-filled process, so do not expect instant growth from the moment of infancy. Instead, plant your children in the nutrient-rich soil of a godly home and trust the Lord to send rain and sun in appropriate measure. Construct aqueducts to divert God's life-giving water to your children, then pray and watch and wait. Even then, growth will not occur until your children learn what it means to die to self (Rom. 6:6) and live for Christ (Gal. 2:20). Only by grace will they bear much fruit.

PRAYER: *Dear Heavenly Father, Show me how to wisely cultivate the soil of our home so that my children will grow up in the discipline and instruction of the Lord. Help me to remember that parenting is a grace-filled process as I* *wait patiently for the harvest. Send the essentials for spiritual growth which only you provide and turn my children to faith in you. In your Son's name, Amen.*

--------------□--------------

Write down one way you will apply today's Proverb:

—11—

PRIDE

Pride goes before destruction,
and a haughty spirit before a fall.
- PROVERBS 16:18

Occasionally, you may read a bumper sticker boasting: "I am the proud parent of an honor student at such-and-such school." Your prideful response may either be, "Psssh! My child is smarter than yours" or "Why don't you just keep that to yourself." I've even seen the bumper sticker rebuke: "My kid can beat up your honor student."

Pride is one of the greatest pitfalls in parenting (Prov. 16:18), for we usually see pride in others before we see it in ourselves. In addition, pride manifests itself with different guises. We may blindly believe that proud people must be boastful, yet arrogance need not be flamboyant. Boasters express their pride aloud, while the bashful keep it in. We can be quiet and reserved, but still be sanctimonious like whiny Moses (Exod. 4:10-14a) instead of hardhearted Pharaoh (v. 21). God tells Moses, "Go," but Moses insists, "I can't!" God tells him, "I have given you everything you need." Moses objects, "I don't think so." At first glance, Moses appears humble, yet God rebukes the fear of man rooted in his pride (Prov. 29:25). Moses thinks too much of himself: "What should I say? What if they don't listen? What if I fail? I'm not very eloquent." In his pride, Moses takes his focus off the Lord even as he stands barefoot in the Lord's holy presence.

So also, dads, you may be concerned that if you don't look out for your family, then no one else will. You believe that you can save your children by good works, instead of grace. You seek the approval of man vicariously through your kids. You are driven by, "What will people think?" rather than, "How does God want me to disciple my children?" Moses only learned humility when he rested his identity in the Lord (Num. 12:3). For humility is not thinking less of yourself, but thinking of yourself less.

During a family dinner at a public restaurant, one of my boys hand-sculpted a volcano out of mashed potatoes and made it erupt with pepperoni lava. Then just as I glanced in his direction, he plunged his face into his plate and devoured the volcano like a rabid dog. I yelped with horror: "No! Stop! Use a fork!" Yet I thought to myself after the trauma: "Why was I horrified?"

It wasn't as the concerned parent: "How is this boy ever going to find a wife?"

It wasn't as the concerned citizen: "Are we disturbing the other diners in this restaurant?"

Rather, I was horrified because of pride: "My barbarian son's manners reflect terribly on me as a parent."

Dads, the way you respond to embarrassment, conflict, criticism, or success depicts the state of your heart. If pride dwells in your heart, then any kind of pressure will force it out (4:23). You do not need to wait, however, for pride to surface. Instead, ask the Lord to illuminate any prideful thoughts or behavior to which you are blind. You need God's help to recognize sin (Ps. 139:23). Then confess both the fruit of your pride and its root. For example, confess your outburst of anger against a misbehaving child and also your people-pleasing heart which led to that prideful response.

Second, cultivate humility by fearing the Lord instead of man (Prov. 29:25). Trust the Father for your own self-worth and the Savior for your children's well-being. Daily gaze upon the cross and humbly recognize the ugliness of sin, for Jesus gave his life so that you might live. He paid the price for undeserving sinners. You cannot be a prideful parent if you keep the cross of Christ continually before you. You will not seek the approval of man or compare yourself with others when you are focused on Christ alone.

PRAYER: *Dear Heavenly Father, I am a prideful parent who often finds my identity and success in the achievements of my children. Help me to entrust my children to you. Let me rejoice in every way you bless them and cling to you in every trial. Teach me to parent for your glory and not for mine. In your Son's name, Amen.*

--------------□--------------

Write down one way you will apply today's Proverb:

—12—

FOLLY

Folly is bound up in the heart of a child,
but the rod of discipline drives it far from him.
- PROVERBS 22:15

Your child is a fool. I hate to break it to you, but your child is a wisdom-rejecting, common sense-shirking, God-denying fool.

One night, my sons devised a new game called *America's Greatest Talent* which required training in their bedroom when they should have been asleep. Course challenges involved scuttling the bookshelf and scaling the bunk bed (without the ladder, of course). The greatest talent was to leap from the top bunk and land on a pillow the size of a postage stamp just inches from the wall (all this in the dark). I walked in on them and found it mildly amusing, but my wife was appalled.

Like most parents, we cannot count the number of times we have spoken with shock: "What in the world were you thinking?" Dads, teach your children wisdom, for they are foolish by nature: "Folly is bound up in the heart of a child, but the rod of discipline drives it far from him" (Prov. 22:15). Young fools, unless instructed wisely, will soon become older fools who remain blind in their sin.

Solomon mourns such naïveté: "I have seen among the simple, I have perceived among the youths, a young man lacking sense, passing along the street near her corner, taking the road to her house. . . . And behold, the woman meets him, dressed as a prostitute, wily of heart" (7:7-8, 10). This woman is dressed to kill, creeping out into the street like a spider from her web. Literally, "she guards her heart" to conceal her intentions. "She is loud" (v. 11a) and boisterous, calling attention to herself. As the life of the party, she's out on the town, seeking a good time while her husband travels abroad (vv. 19-20). This wayward wife rebels against her husband: "Her feet do not stay at home; now in the street, now in the market, and at every corner she lies in wait" (vv. 11b-12). She prowls everywhere looking for trouble, yet finds a fool delivered to her very doorstep. Quickly she pounces: "She seizes him and kisses him" (v. 13a). With shocking boldness, she pulls him close and plants a wet one on his lips. Unabashed, this brazen hussy breaks her marriage vows in public. Her mouth drips with temptation (vv. 13b-18) and this is just one of many enticements your foolish child will face.

Dads, "train up a child in the way he should go" (22:6a) implies that you are to train your child in godliness. Yet this is not a guaranteed promise of good children, but rather a warning against child-centered parenting. The Hebrew text does not specify whose way your child must follow: "The way of the Lord," "the way that is right," or, "the way according to Scripture." It simply states, "Start out a child according to his way," and in Proverbs, "his way," usually means, "the way that the person chooses." In other words, "Don't let your child choose his own stubborn way or when he grows up he will still be foolish." The wise father does not counsel his son to do whatever he feels, but instead warns him of what will happen if he does.

Young children especially need your instruction since they are born foolish. Their own way is full of folly and dangerous to the soul. If you let them rule the house like little kings and queens, their sinful hearts will choose the wrong way every time. So spare your children with loving, godly discipline (v. 15b). Instruct them according to God's Word, expose the dangers of sin, and warn against the consequences. Discipline appropriately when they disobey, then trust the Lord to remove the folly in their hearts.

PRAYER: *Dear Heavenly Father, I am parenting fools who do not always follow the way of wisdom. Teach me to be wise according to your Word as I show them your path (Ps. 119:105). Change my heart as you employ me to help change theirs. Make me a father who lovingly and appropriately applies the tool of discipline to lead my children into a relationship with you. In your Son's name, Amen.*

--------------□--------------

Write down one way you will apply today's Proverb:

13

ANXIETY

Anxiety in a man's heart weighs him down,
but a good word makes him glad.
- PROVERBS 12:25

I was lost, driving through an unfamiliar neighborhood when my GPS died. I looked around my car, but could not locate a single map. (Yes, there was a day when maps were made of paper.) I get anxious when I don't know where I'm driving, so I began to feel a headache and a terrible feeling in my stomach. I was also running low on gas and late for an appointment. Then I had a second appointment after that one, which I would probably miss as well and have to pay late fees. My fear started spinning out of control and at that moment, another car blocked my lane. I missed my turn and found myself getting agitated at a complete stranger. Anxiety became a downward spiral as my sinful responses increased life's pressures. This rapid descent, dads, will eventually lead to a crash, so squelch your anxiety as soon as it begins.

I first had to take responsibility for my sin. The problem wasn't the driver in front of me, the poor signage, or my phone's dead battery. I had to accept my fault for responding with anxiety. My circumstances explained my sin, but did not excuse it. Second, I had to recognize my selfish heart and ask the Lord to forgive me. I was so focused on myself that I hadn't been thinking about others: "How were my actions affecting them?" "How could I be a more courteous driver?" "How could I set a godly example for my son in the back seat?" I confessed my heart of anxiety which had led to anger, impatience, and lack of trust. I confessed my selfish craving for comfort and not wanting to be inconvenienced. I also confessed my love of money at trying to escape late fees and my fear of man: "What will people think if I'm late?"

Then once I put off my fear and my heart idolatry, I had to put on love for God and love for others (Matt. 22:36-40). I had to say, "No!" to fear and

"Yes!" to God. So I prayed, "Lord, how I can honor you in the midst of my anxiety? How can I serve the people around me instead of focusing on myself?" I had to take captive the barbarians in my mind (2 Cor. 10:5) and replace those irrational fears with biblical thoughts (Phil. 4:8)—not simply optimistic ones.

"*So what if I'm late? What if I'm lost*?" "God is still in control: 'The heart of man plans his way, but the LORD establishes his steps'" (Prov. 16:9).

"*What about that dumb driver in front of me? Don't I have the right to be angry*?" "No, actually I don't: 'For the anger of man does not produce the righteousness of God'" (Jas. 1:20).

"*What if I lose time or money because my car runs out of gas or I have to reschedule*?" "Remember Matthew 6:33, 'But seek first the kingdom of God and his righteousness, and all these things will be added to you.'"

"*What if I lose face because I miss my appointment*? 'The LORD is on my side; I will not fear. What can man do to me?' (Ps. 118:6). The overarching purpose of my life, even in trials, is to become more like Christ each day" (Rom. 8:28-29).

Despite my feelings, I had to believe the truth and act in faith (Phil. 4:9). My driving became less erratic and my attitude more patient (v. 5a). I asked my son, "Would you pray with daddy?" (vv. 5b-7). I treated others on the road with kindness even though my earlier desire had been to run them over. Then as I acted in faith, my feelings of anxiety began to diminish. Praise God, I didn't get lost or run out of gas. I made it to my first appointment slightly late and the second one actually cancelled on me. It all worked out. But even if it didn't, God was doing something bigger in my heart.

Dads, anxiety will drive you to helplessness as you parent your children. Consider this list of top ten fears for new dads:

1. Does my baby have health complications?
2. What if the pregnancy goes wrong?
3. What if I don't know what to do? Will I mess up my kid?
4. What if I drop him?
5. Is she getting any sleep? Am I getting any sleep?
6. Why won't he quit crying?
7. What if she refuses to eat? What if she eats too much?

8. Will my wife stop wanting to be intimate?
9. What if we can't pay the bills?
10. What if I'm not a good dad?

Fatherhood provides ample opportunities to be anxious, so let your helplessness drive you closer to the Lord as you fight anxiety with Philippians 4:

1. Rejoice in the Lord (v. 4a).
2. Rejoice in the Lord again (v. 4b).
3. Act responsibly and use common sense (v. 5a).
4. Trust that God is always with you (v. 5b).
5. Do not be anxious (v. 6a).
6. Pray with both supplication and thanksgiving (v. 6b).
7. Experience God's peace in your heart and mind (v. 7).
8. Take anxious thoughts captive with biblical thoughts (v. 8).
9. Practice what you have learned from godly mentors (v. 9a).
10. Practice what you have learned in Scripture (v. 9b).

PRAYER: *Dear Heavenly Father, I am anxious about so many things. I struggle with my barbarian thoughts and need to trust in you. Help me to recognize my fears and replace them with biblical wisdom. Show me the peace that passes all understanding even in the midst of the most difficult times. In your Son's name, Amen.*

-------------□-------------

Write down one way you will apply today's Proverb:

14

ANGER

Whoever is slow to anger is better than the mighty,
and he who rules his spirit than he who takes a city.
- PROVERBS 16:32

Children often breathe their parents' second-hand anger. At my son's back-to-school night, I noticed one student's artwork with the entire page scribbled in red crayon. The teacher asked, "*What's that a picture of*?" The little boy answered, "It's my daddy. He's really, really mad."

Dads, your children are fools who will often offend you (Prov. 22:15), yet you must learn to control your anger or you will destroy your home and your relationship with your children (25:28). Anger wrongly frames discipline as a problem between parent and child, thus teaching them to fear man instead of the Lord (29:25). Instead of exposing your children's sin, it makes them emotional weathermen: "What kind of mood is daddy in right now? How much can I get away with?" Your children learn to appease you because they long for a stable environment, yet anger will destroy your family from within. So consider the wisdom of Proverbs: "Good sense makes one slow to anger, and it is his glory to overlook an offense" (19:11).

One night, two of my boys were horsing around, spoon-fighting at dinner (for the uninitiated, that's sword-fighting with spoons), when they both fell off their chairs. It's ridiculous the number of times in our home that little boys have fallen off their chairs in the middle of dinner. This particular meal took an hour longer than necessary as I repeatedly reprimanded them to finish eating. I was about to yell in frustration, but I had to check myself. My desires had morphed into demands. They had gone from "I want" to "I must have" until those demands ruled my heart. I began to view my desire for respectful children and for peace and quiet as something I deserved—rewards for a life well-lived: "I work so hard to take care of these kids. I put food on their plates. I'm not asking for much. I deserve their respect. I demand their respect." Yet the moment my desires drifted into demands, they became sinful heart idolatry. Idols are not simply statues of wood and stone, but anything I depend on apart from God for happiness or security. An idol is whatever I love and pursue more than God.

Dads, which desires rule your heart? Will you sin in order to get them or sin if they are withheld? If so, you have an idol. Pay attention and your anger will expose your heart. One helpful practice is to journal any occasion you get sinfully angry this week:

1. Write down what happened. Summarize the situation.
2. Admit you lost control in anger: "A man without self-control is like a city broken into and left without walls" (Prov. 25:28).
3. Then ask yourself: "What did I say, do, and feel in that situation?" Record your words, behavior, and emotions (especially when sinful).
4. Most importantly, examine the source of your anger: "What were my thoughts and desires at the time? What was I wanting or defending that led to my anger?"
5. Repent not just for sinful anger, but also for sinful heart desires (28:13) since you must pluck out the weed by its root. Don't waste your anger. Instead, pay close attention and root out the idols of your heart.

Anger contaminates your deepest roots, yet thankfully the gospel goes deeper. So let the Lord transform your sinful heart and enable you to apply the Proverbs: "A soft answer turns away wrath, but a harsh word stirs up anger" (15:1) and "a hot-tempered man stirs up strife, but he who is slow to anger quiets contention" (v. 18). Also "if your enemy is hungry, give him bread to eat, and if he is thirsty, give him water to drink" (25:21; see 24:17-18) and "whoever is slow to anger is better than the mighty, and he who rules his spirit than he who takes a city" (16:32). Seek to emulate the patient lovingkindness which the Lord has shown to you.

Dads, just as you would never smoke celebratory cigars over your baby's crib, so also snuff out your anger (Ps. 37:8a; Col. 3:8). Focus on character qualities and godly actions to put on in place of anger: self-control (Prov.

16:32; 25:28; 29:11; Gal. 5:23), edifying speech (Prov. 10:11, 13, 19-21, 31-32; 12:18, 25; 15:1; Eph. 4:25-32), and biblical peacemaking (Matt. 5:9; Rom. 12:18; 14:19). Put on gentleness, patience, and humility (Jas. 1:19): "What new thoughts should I be thinking? What is the right goal for right now? How can I be patient and consider the interests of others? How can I serve God and the people around me? Is there something productive I can do about this problem?" Allow Scripture you have memorized to transform your thoughts. Keep fighting the battle against anger until you can claim the victory.

PRAYER: *Dear Heavenly Father, Convict me of any anger in my own heart. Show me how to reject this deadly sin and put on the character of Christ. Teach me to speak with gentle and edifying words even when I feel frustrated by my circumstances. Then help me to model Christ's patient lovingkindness toward my children instead of provoking them to anger. In your Son's name, Amen.*

--------------□--------------

Write down one way you will apply today's Proverb:

—15—

LAZINESS

Go to the ant, O sluggard;
Consider her ways, and be wise.
- PROVERBS 6:6

The first week after bringing home a newborn is always difficult. For one of our boys, my wife woke up every two hours to nurse and woke me up as well to share in her misery. My job was to lift our son from the bassinet, hand him to my wife, then fall asleep until it was time to replace our bundle of joy. (I'm convinced that caring for a newborn is a kind of sleep torture to condition parents for the rigors of childrearing.) After just a few of those evening exercises, I became so disoriented when my wife woke me that I would have to ask, "Coming or going?" Thankfully, after the first couple weeks, my wife realized that I was not an essential cog in the late-night feedings. (I had figured that out much earlier, but was wise enough not to verbalize it.) I slept so soundly during that first night of uninterrupted bliss that I asked her the next morning, "Oh, did he sleep through the night?" My wife was not at all amused.

The sluggard is also a heavy sleeper who turns on his bed "as a door turns on its hinges" (Prov. 26:14). Yet dads, the hard work of parenting is not for the lazy. Those first weeks (or months) of late-night feedings are nothing in comparison to the rest of your child's life. God has called you to labor for your child in earnest prayer, loving discipline, wise instruction, joyful relationship, and quality time. Every day, you are called to shepherd your child whether you feel like it or not. You can't return him to the store, get your money back, or take a "daddy day" off.

My boys love to recite Proverbs 6:6 with gusto: "Go to the ant, O sluggard; consider her ways, and be wise." The tiny ant is, first of all, self-disciplined: "Without having any chief, officer, or ruler" (v. 7). She is tireless without a taskmaster—ambitious without an administrator. Likewise, dads, are you disciplined? Do you start your tasks immediately or do you delay because of perceived obstacles? Are you reading your Bible, praying faithfully, and leading your family to follow Christ? Unlike the ant, the sluggard thinks only of self. He is the husband who peels his rear end from the couch only when his wife explodes. He might be selectively lazy—busy at work and sluggard at home. Dads, do not wait for someone else to tell you what to do. Instead, serve the Lord with ant-like self-discipline.

Second, the ant provides for the future: "She prepares her bread in summer and gathers her food in harvest" (v. 8), for she knows that indolence today means starvation tomorrow. She does not squander summer, for winter soon approaches (see 30:25). Men, when you pursued marriage, you found a job to provide for your wife. You started saving for more than just your personal needs and learned how to give generously to others. You worked hard at your job "to the glory of God" (1 Cor. 10:31b) and to provide for your family's future. Your diligence must reflect your foresight.

The third lesson the ant teaches is to be wisely industrious. Is your work motivated by selfish pride, the tyranny of the urgent, or the love of pleasure? Perhaps you view work so you can rest, yet the Bible instructs you to rest so you can work (Exod. 20:8-10). Work has dignity as ordained by God from creation (Gen. 2:15). It is good and noble, reflecting God's glory (Col. 3:23-24). Work has been hard ever since the Fall (Gen. 3:17-19), yet these challenges should lead you to depend even more on God.

Solomon then continues: "How long will you lie there, O sluggard? When will you arise from your sleep? A little sleep, a little slumber, a little folding of the hands to rest" (Prov. 6:9-10). The question, "How long?" indicates lengthy indolence, for the sluggard moves like syrup in the freezer—slow as molasses. How long will you be "looking" for work? How long will you fill your evenings with meaningless activity? How long will you remain a nominal churchgoer who does not intentionally make disciples? How long, O sluggard, will you be set in your ways? The repetition demands an answer so as to wake him from his lethargy.

Sadly, the sluggard creeps in every one of us. He falls asleep at home, paralyzed by inactivity. His hands are idle or glued to the iPhone. Do not be the sluggard or "poverty will come upon you like a robber, and want like an armed man" (v. 11; see 24:30-34).

I love my boys and desire each of them to grow in wisdom, learn God's

Word, and follow after Christ. I pray they find a job, pursue a wife, and eventually own a place they call home. I don't want them waking up on my couch one day, realizing they have wasted the precious life God gave them. Dads, teach your children to be diligent today or they will reap the sluggard's consequences.

PRAYER: *Dear Heavenly Father, Teach me to work hard at the task of fatherhood. Give me delight in the work and joy in the harvest. Grant me a vision of godly children ministering to others and working hard to exalt your glory. Then remove the sluggard both in me and in my children. In your Son's name, Amen.*

---------------□--------------

Write down one way you will apply today's Proverb:

16

SPEECH

Death and life are in the power of the tongue,
and those who love it will eat its fruits.
- PROVERBS 18:21

While reading *The Pilgrim's Progress* as a family, we came upon the characters Faithful and Talkative. "What is Talkative's personality?" one son asked.

"He talks a lot," I answered, "Do you think that's good or bad?"

Thinking for a moment, he replied noncommittally, "Well, he could be a pastor."

I suppose many a pastor could be characterized as talkative, yet every one of us must examine our speech. Words have the power of "death and life" (Prov. 18:21), to hurt and to heal, to wreck and restore. We can harm a neighbor with deception (25:18), anger (29:22), gossip or slander (16:27-28), babbling words (15:2b; 21:23; 29:20), flattery (29:5), and scoffing (29:8a). Yet the struggle is not in our vocal chords or on our lips, because word problems reveal heart problems (Luke 6:45). The mouth is merely the tunnel through which depravity escapes (Matt. 15:18-19). For this reason, Proverbs often connects the heart with speech. Only after you guard your heart (Prov. 4:23), will you "put away from you crooked speech, and put devious talk far from you" (v. 24).

Dads, you may try to shift the blame: "You made me angry." "I only lied because I felt trapped." "I couldn't help myself." "I didn't mean to say those words." Yet you cannot blame your speech on the people or circumstances around you. Those influences simply trigger the occasion for your heart to reveal itself in words. So in addition to removing those triggers, you must receive a transformed heart. Communication is not primarily a skill to be learned, but a matter of worship. The one who holds your heart is the one your words will honor.

Now you cannot accomplish this godly communication by human effort (see 20:9; Jas. 3:5-8), but only by the supernatural power of Christ—the Living Word (John 1:14). Christ alone grants the hope of a transformed heart (Ezek. 36:25-27), the riches of every spiritual blessing in the heavenly places (Eph. 1:3), and divine power granting to you all things pertaining to life and godliness (2 Pet. 1:3). Christ alone is the sovereign King who rules not only the entire universe, but also your heart and tongue. He rose from the dead and was appointed Ruler of all, so he can certainly empower you to speak with grace (Rom. 8:11).

Dads, the only way to gain victory over speech is to acknowledge Christ as Lord. Begin by trusting in his sovereign plan (Prov. 16:1-4), for no situation, circumstance, or relationship escapes his charge. He rules your life, directing all things for his glory and your redemptive good (Rom. 8:28). This good news exhorts you to examine your words regularly in the mirror of God's Word (Jas. 1:22-25). Take time to study Proverbs and evaluate your communication: "Are my speech patterns godly or self-serving?" The kindness of God will convict your heart of sinful motives and lead you to repent. The war of words is a war of worship, because whoever rules your heart will control the words you speak.

Perhaps, however, you feel defeated in your struggle with speech. You play back the recording of this past week and hear yourself using profane or unkind words. Begin by humbly recognizing that your sinful speech arises from an idolatrous heart. You lie and cheat, complain and quarrel, implode and explode as you defend your kingdom of self. You flatter and cajole, manipulate and sweeten, and say what people want to benefit the kingdom in your heart. For example, I might speak harshly to my children out of impatience. They're making me late, disrupting my comfort, or not respecting my authority. My children are not submitting to my kingship in the home. In those moments, I must confess my impatient heart: "Lord, I have not been trusting you as sovereign in my family and in my home. Lord, you are in control. You sovereignly ordained these unruly rugrats for my sanctification and their instruction. Lord, forgive my selfish heart and my impatient speech."

Once you confess the heart behind the struggle, then commit to godly change. Ask yourself pointed questions:

- Do I speak from a compassionate heart?
- Do people characterize my speech as kind and

humble, patient and meek?

- Do I tend to attack or forgive?
- Am I grateful or grumbling?
- Are my words seeped in Christ-like love?
- Do I do all things, in word and deed, to the glory of Christ (Col. 3:17)?

Christ can transform you into his ambassador who will speak not your own words, but the message of your King (2 Cor. 5:11-21). You will enter every conversation asking, "How can I glorify God and serve this other person?" "How can I be an ambassador for Christ?" Each word you speak is a witness for Jesus, so speak words that help instead of harm. Meditate on God's Word to change your words (Prov. 10:11, 21; 11:30; 12:6, 18, 25; 13:14; 15:1, 18, 23, 28; 16:20-24; 18:4; 21:23; 25:11-12; 27:5-6, 9, 11-12). The goal of godly speech is to glorify Christ and to serve the people around you (Eph. 4:29).

PRAYER: *Dear Heavenly Father, Transform my heart and reform my speech. Guard my tongue from sin and teach me to communicate only edifying words. Show me how to be a right representative of your kingdom and to only express the message of my King. In your Son's name, Amen.*

--------------□--------------

Write down one way you will apply today's Proverb:

17

DECEPTION

Lying lips are an abomination to the LORD,
but those who act faithfully are his delight.
- PROVERBS 12:22

Children often lie for fear of discipline. My son once blamed his brother for drawing with chalk on the neighbor's driveway, so I had to explain that his deception concerned me more than his colorful scribbles. "Tell me the truth," I told him, "You won't be disciplined for your artwork, but only if you lie to me." Tearfully, my son confessed his sin and sought his brother's forgiveness.

In biblical times, silver workers would heat the precious metal to a boil, then skim the impurities from the surface. Merchants would then recycle that dross as decorative glaze to coat their pottery. Their earthen vessels would sparkle and shine like silver, though possessing little value. So also are "fervent lips with an evil heart" (Prov. 26:23-26), for sparkling speech and flattering tongues can easily deceive. Thankfully, dads, your children are often poor liars, so their deception is easily caught. The greater challenge, however, is to patiently instruct them afterward. Do not simply aim for changed behavior, but shepherd their hearts to stop telling lies and to start encouraging others (Eph. 4:25).

The first lie echoed loudly in a paradise designed by God. The Creator had spoken the universe into existence (Gen. 1:3), beauty into the garden, and wise counsel into the hearts of Adam and Eve: "I love you and will provide. I will give you good gifts" (see 2:16-17).

Soon after, however, God's voice was not alone as the serpent voiced the words of Satan: "God doesn't love you. He's keeping the best to himself. Look at that delicious fruit and imagine the wisdom you will gain. You will not surely die" (see 3:4-5). Adam and his wife were forced to choose between competing voices. Yet the war was not in the words, but deep within their hearts (v. 6; Prov. 12:20a). For a lie is never just a lie, but an act of worship.

Dads, consider the life-or-death consequences of telling the truth:

"A man of crooked heart does not discover good, and one with a dishonest tongue falls into calamity" (17:20; see 19:5).

You may reach the ends of the earth by lying, but you will never get back. You may get away with deception in the moment, yet only truth builds lasting character (see 12:19).

Deceitful practices are like chewing on a mouthful of gravel as the grit grinds against your conscience (see 20:17).

Lying not only harms you personally, but also those you love (see 18:21). It destroys relationships from within, ruins reputations, and breaks the hard-earned trust you had with others (see 3:32).

Most crucially, deception grieves the Lord:
"Lying lips are an abomination to the LORD,
but those who act faithfully are his delight" (12:22).
Dishonesty brings dishonor, for God loves truth and hates deception. He despises any distortion of his character (see 21:12; 24:12) and will ultimately make all things right (Rom. 12:19).

Our world too often stops at moralism instead of continuing on to the gospel destination. They recognize the natural consequences that "deception harms both you and others," but then they reason, "Harmless lies are fine. Little fibs will go unnoticed." They fail to understand that we fight the battle for words on the soil of our hearts. They do not see that every lie disparages the God of truth, every deceit distorts the reflection of his glory, and just one falsehood before an infinitely holy God condemns a soul to hell for all eternity.

The gospel, however, declares that we face judgment for denying the truth about God's goodness and our need for a Savior. The gospel tells the truth about sin—that we have fallen short of God's holy standard. The gospel exposes our former manner of life and corruption "through deceitful desires." The gospel goes beyond behavioral modification, because the power to change is: "to be renewed in the spirit of your minds" (Eph. 4:22-24). The only way for a liar to become a truth-teller is to receive a changed heart and the only path to a changed heart is the truth about Jesus fully displayed in the gospel (see John 14:6).

You might instruct your child, "I'm concerned that you've been telling lies, so let me remind you of the gospel. We worship a holy God who created us to truthfully reflect his glory by the way we speak. Yet sadly, sin entered the world and now corrupts our selfish desires. Even one tiny lie deserves the penalty of eternal judgment, so God sent his Son to pay that price upon the cross. We were unable to save ourselves, but Jesus died to forgive our sin. Rejoice with me in Christ's resurrection power over sin and death. Praise the Lord for his power to turn liars into truth-tellers. God will adopt us into his family and make us joint heirs with Christ. This is the wonderful privilege of belonging to the church—the mystery of God which has now been revealed" (see Eph. 1-3).

Dads, daily impart these gospel truths in bite-sized pieces, so that when you address the problem of deception you have already prepared your children well. Teach them to lovingly speak the truth to fellow believers with whom they are united in Christ (4:25). Motivate them not by fear of punishment, fear of failure, or fear of man, but by the love of Christ (2 Cor. 5:14-15). The gospel alone can change their hearts and lead to changed behavior. Anything less is silver glaze on an earthen vessel.

PRAYER: *Dear Heavenly Father, I constantly seek to hide my sin, deceiving you and others. So often, I forget the gospel truth that I am forgiven and pardoned from judgment. Teach me to speak edifying words to build up fellow Christians. Show me how to put away deception and honor you with honesty. In your Son's name, Amen.*

--------------□--------------

Write down one way you will apply today's Proverb:

18

DISCONTENTMENT

Whoever trusts in his riches will fall,
but the righteous will flourish like a green leaf.
- PROVERBS 11:28

My wife once traveled to Arizona and asked my son what he wanted for a gift.

He replied, “I’d like a snake.” (We were reading Genesis and his favorite Bible character was the serpent.)

I pressed him, “You mean like a pretend snake.”

“No,” he insisted, “A real snake.”

Needless to say he was disappointed (for about three seconds).

We all experience disappointment in life, so Paul explains the key to contentment: “Not that I am speaking of being in need, for I have learned in whatever situation I am to be content. I know how to be brought low, and I know how to abound. In any and every circumstance, I have learned the secret of facing plenty and hunger, abundance and need. I can do all things through him who strengthens me” (Phil. 4:11-13). Contentment requires trusting the sovereign God to set our expectations rightly.

My wife and I often talk with our children about making wise financial decisions. We pray together as a family over sacrifices like downsizing our home, helping others in need, or supporting missionaries. We often encourage one another: “Better is a dinner of herbs where love is than a fattened ox and hatred with it” (Prov. 15:17; see 17:1). We prioritize cherishing our family before storing away wealth. For money is not wrong to have, but as J. C. Ryle wrote in *Riches and Poverty*, “Money is one of the most unsatisfying of possessions. It takes away some cares, no doubt; but brings with it quite as many cares. There is trouble in getting it, anxiety in keeping it, temptations in using it, guilt in abusing it, sorrow in losing it, and perplexity in disposing of it.”

In Proverbs 30, King Agur makes a humble request of the Lord:

"Two things I ask of you; deny them not to me before I die:
Remove far from me falsehood and lying;
give me neither poverty nor riches" (vv. 7-8a).
Do not make me either too rich or too poor,
but "feed me with the food that is needful for me,
lest I be full and deny you and say, 'Who is the LORD?' or lest I be poor and steal and profane the name of my God" (vv. 8b-9).

Agur wisely centers his heart upon the Lord:

O Lord, do not make me overly rich.
Provide only the food I need each day or
I will grow proud in my prosperity.
I might believe the lie that I don't need you—
that I can make it on my own (see 11:28).
I might turn my wealth into an idol.
But also, Lord, do not make me overly poor.
Provide my daily bread or
I will grow desperate in my poverty (see 6:30).
I might believe the lie that you don't care—
that I've got to make it on my own.
I might turn my fear into an idol.
O Lord, give me neither poverty nor riches.

Let me not be the fool who claims, "There is no God" (Ps. 14:1)
and profanes the name of God: "Who is the Lord?"
Instead, turn my heart to yours and prove true your every word:
"For who is God, but the LORD?
And who is a rock, except our God" (18:31)?

Dads, you might rephrase Agur's prayer to be your own: "O Lord, grant me only what is needful to make me more like Jesus."

Give me trials or give me rest;
Give me only what is best.
Make me rich or make me poor;
Whichever way just make me more like Jesus.

PRAYER: *Dear Heavenly Father, Teach me to be content when my wandering heart keeps looking for more. Help me to rest in your all-sufficient arms and trust that you will provide whatever we need. Then show me how to pass on this legacy of contentment, so that my children will cling to you in every circumstance. In your Son's name, Amen.*

--------------□--------------

Write down one way you will apply today's Proverb:

19

TEMPTATION

Can a man carry fire next to his chest and his clothes not be burned?
Or can one walk on hot coals and his feet not be scorched?
So is he who goes in to his neighbor's wife;
none who touches her will go unpunished.
- PROVERBS 6:27-29

Dads, it is good to warn your children about poison oak: "See that oily bush, son. That's poison oak. Leaves of three, let it be." Yet what if you were not sure what poison oak looked like? You might carelessly walk right into it and lead your children through it also. Or else you might be overprotective: "Don't touch anything green!" Your children would go through life petrified of nature. Yet even more importantly, you must warn your children against temptation. Warn them what to watch out for and what to do when they are pressured. If you do not instruct them, someone else will.

Solomon, for example, warns his son about the adulteress: "The lips of a forbidden woman drip honey, and her speech is smoother than oil, but in the end she is bitter as wormwood, sharp as a two-edged sword. Her feet go down to death; her steps follow the path to Sheol; she does not ponder the path of life; her ways wander, and she does not know it" (Prov. 5:3-6). Solomon knows that if he keeps silent about sex because of shame or fear, his son may end up scared or repressed or deviant about a gift which God designed as good.

You may not need to have this "talk" until they are older, but still you must teach the whole counsel of Scripture in an age-appropriate way. For example, when I studied Proverbs with my boys they would always laugh about the forbidden woman: "Beware the forbidden woman, hahaha." They didn't know a thing about adultery, but they knew enough to stay away from her. Occasionally they would even call out the forbidden woman when they saw a female villain in a movie: Captain Phasma, Ursula the sea urchin,

Cruella de Vil, or those wicked step-sisters of Cinderella. Right now, my boys need only know that some women are evil and some are virtuous, yet we have laid the foundation for future conversations.

Dads, do not give clearer warnings about poison oak than about spiritual temptations your children will face. The watchful father knows the danger of prideful naïveté: "I have seen among the simple, I have perceived among the youths, a young man lacking sense" (7:7)—a fool out for an evening stroll without God's Word on the tablet of his heart (1:4). His companions also are simpleminded—vain men without conviction who watch him stride foolishly into danger (13:20).

This youth spurns his father's warning and arrogantly declares, "That will not ever happen to me." He has no plan to spare his purity, but is "open-minded" to adultery. He has failed to establish his convictions before temptation comes (see Job 31:1). Suddenly, he finds himself in the wrong place at the wrong time: "Passing along the street near her corner, taking the road to her house in the twilight, in the evening, at the time of night and darkness" (Prov. 7:8-9). He ambles down her street and passes by her door at twilight. The darkness hides his shameful intentions. Every step draws him closer to her house, for he lives on the edge of temptation. He flirts with danger: "It can't hurt. How can something that feels so good be wrong?"

Solomon, however, proposes a better way: "And now, O sons, listen to me, and be attentive to the words of my mouth. Let not your heart turn aside to her ways; do not stray into her paths, for many a victim has she laid low, and all her slain are a mighty throng. Her house is the way to Sheol, going down to the chambers of death" (vv. 24-27).

Dads, you cannot determine your child's every choice, but you can warn him against temptation. Alert him to the dangers and set him on the righteous path. Show her the blessings of a God-pleasing life so she will have no reason to crouch outside sin's door. She must not find her rush from dangerous living and tempting temptation. Instead, may she delight to do God's will and find her abundant life in him.

PRAYER: *Dear Heavenly Father, My children will face much temptation in this fallen world. Teach me to wisely warn them of danger and to establish biblical convictions in advance. Help me not to fall into temptation myself and to set for them a godly example. In your Son's name, Amen.*

--------------□--------------

Write down one way you will apply today's Proverb:

—20—

CONDUCT

Even a child makes himself known by his acts,
by whether his conduct is pure and upright.
- PROVERBS 20:11

Imagine, if you will, an apple tree in your backyard. The branches, which once boasted lush foliage, are now withered and bare. The sickly trunk leans off to one side. The fruit, once plentiful, has fallen to the ground to rot. Think how foolish it would be to approach that tree with a ladder, a staple gun, and a bucket full of red delicious apples. If you tried to staple those apples to that sickly tree, they would rot within days because the problem is the root and not the fruit (Mark 7:21-23; Luke 6:43-45).

So also, dads, your child's sinful conduct begins in the heart. You can paint the fruit of their behavior red as much as you like, but a sinful heart makes that an exercise in futility (Jer. 17:9). The "heart" describes the inner person—the center of their being (Mark 12:30). As your child's central processing unit, it controls the mind (Prov. 23:7; Eph. 1:18), emotions (Pss. 37:4; 111:1; Prov. 13:12), and will (Eph. 6:6; Heb. 4:12; 10:22).

Jesus also described the heart as the birthplace of sin and rebuked the religious leaders for painting fruit on dead branches (Mark 7:1). They were the model citizens at the temple any time the gates were open. They were meticulous about Bible study, tithing, and service. Jesus, however, exposed their rotten roots as he quoted from the prophet Isaiah: "This people honors me with their lips, but their heart is far from me; in vain do they worship me, teaching as doctrines the commandments of men" (vv. 6-7; see Isa. 29:13). All sin, whether legalism or lawlessness—man-made religion or secular humanism, originates in the heart. So dads, do not raise Pharisees who conduct themselves morally, but are rotten at the core. Hope in God to change your children's hearts such that their transformed hearts will lead to godly conduct.

The ideal Jewish family was seven sons since seven was the number of perfection and sons were more profitable than daughters in that culture (see Ruth 4:15). So when my wife and I discovered our third child was another boy, I joked with her: "We are 3/7 of the way to the perfect family."

To this she replied, "I guess we're settling for less than perfect."

Dads, take joy in however many children the Lord grants you (Ps. 127:3), but realize that no family is perfect. Those little vipers in diapers will quickly break your trust. So first, hope in God and not your children. Parenting reprobates is risky. You cannot control independent moral agents who are born as sinners and surrounded by rebels. In fact, Proverbs reveals that every child makes his own choice to either walk in wisdom or in folly (4:18-19). Plead with your children to live rightly as you show them the path of wisdom (1:8). Clarify the consequences of choosing either righteousness or sin (20:11), then trust the Lord to change their hearts.

Second, hope in God and not your children's environment. If you make an idol of creating the ideal home or discovering the perfect childrearing strategy, then you will live your life for that idolatrous desire. You will obsess to achieve it and angrily defend it, then despair when it fails and blame God for your suffering. Do not try to sovereignly control your home environment, for you are not the sovereign God. Do not trust in music lessons, homeschooling, youth group, or any other human influence to save your children apart from Christ. Consider Cain, whose parents walked with God. Cain had no peer pressure, video games, or the trappings of today, yet still he murdered his brother in cold blood (e.g., Gen. 4). Work hard to cultivate a loving home environment and to give your children life's advantages, but trust the Lord to change their hearts.

Lastly, hope in God and not yourself. Even if parenting was a formula, every one of us would fall short (Rom. 3:23). "For we all stumble in many ways" (Jas. 3:2). Even if you parent perfectly according to God's way, your children still make independent choices (see Isa. 30:1; Matt 26:14-16). So dads, you are called to parent your children biblically (Prov. 19:18), but yield the results to the sovereign God who alone can change their hearts (10:28).

PRAYER: *Dear Heavenly Father, Let me hope in you and nothing else when I am tempted to idolize my children or exalt my ability to change them. Show me that you alone can change the heart and bring them to salvation. In you* *alone, O Lord, I place my hope. In your Son's name, Amen.*

--------------□--------------

Write down one way you will apply today's Proverb:

—21—

MARRIAGE

Let your fountain be blessed,
and rejoice in the wife of your youth.
- PROVERBS 5:18

Our boys always get a kick out of certain Proverbs. For example, "It is better to live in a corner of the housetop than in a house shared with a quarrelsome wife" (21:9). "It is better to live in a desert land than with a quarrelsome and fretful woman" (v. 19).

"*Why don't you want to live in a desert*?" "Because it's hot."

"*Why don't you want to live on the corner of the roof*?" "It might rain."

"*Why don't you want to live with a quarrelsome wife*?" "Because she will make you sad."

"*Did you know that some mommies and daddies fight all the time*?" "Really?"

It struck me as we were talking that my boys did not even know what a quarrelsome or contentious woman looked like. I thank the Lord for my gracious wife who has given them no cause to revile God's Word (Titus 2:5).

Men, marry wisely so that your children can see their parents live out the practical reality of faith in God. Marry well so that lost sinners may be enticed by the gospel ministry of your family life. May they see Jesus when they look at your love for one another (John 13:34-35). The strength of your marriage can be the greatest testimony of Christ to your children.

Marriage began as God's idea with an eligible bachelor named Adam (Gen. 2:7-8). Adam had a perfectly-sculpted body and a superior intellect untainted by sin. He never had to work out to stay in shape and if he had worn clothes they would have always fit. Adam had hair in all the places he wanted and none in the places he didn't. Nothing sagged, stretched, or ached when he woke up in the morning. He was never plagued by sickness, disease, or even death. Most importantly though, Adam had an intimate relationship with his Creator and a life of rest in a luxurious garden (vv. 9-16). He walked with God every day and talked with him on a personal level. Sure he might have been unemployed, yet he had plenty of work to do (v. 15). In the beginning, Adam was the most eligible man on the planet.

Yet surprisingly, for the first time in the creation week, God said that something was "not good." The language was extremely strong: "NOT GOOD it is that the man should be alone!" (v. 18a). This did not mean that creation was somehow imperfect, but simply unfinished. Man was created for relationship. Even though Adam lived in a perfect paradise with his Creator, a whole zoo of pets, and more organic fruit than a farmer's market, God still said, "It is not good." For man had been created with the ability to speak, the capacity for language, and the means for social interaction. He also had reproductive organs and the charge to be fruitful and multiply and fill the earth (1:28). In the beginning, God had made the man for marriage.

Now, of course, God did not create Mr. and Mrs. Hippo and Mr. and Mrs. Giraffe and Mr. and Mrs. Orangutan, but forget to create the woman. Rather, he had made Adam first to intentionally highlight the man's missing "rib" and to set apart Eve as a special creation. "Then the LORD God said, 'It is not good that the man should be alone; I will make him a helper fit for him'" (2:18)—a suitable helper and corresponding counterpart. The woman was no servant, but a partner—not the man's clone, but his complement—not his weaker half, but the one who supplied strength where he was lacking. The word "helper" was in no way derogative, but rather meant to elevate the woman's status. The same term often described God as the "Helper" of his people (Pss. 10:14; 118:7; see Heb. 13:6).

My wife, Amanda, has been my helper all throughout our marriage. She encourages me, supports me, and speaks the truth when I need to hear it. We talk about almost everything and her words mean more to me that anyone else's. We also have a lot of fun together: talking, laughing, and cherishing our family. Like the first bachelor, I would be all work and no play, but my wife makes sure that we enjoy life. She lights up our house such that I would be lost without her. She is my helper who fits me perfectly. Finding such a wife was hard work, but ultimately a gift of God.

Before I got married, I knew from Scripture that God wanted me to find a Christian woman who loved the Lord (2 Cor. 6:14) and who attracted me both physically and emotionally—a wife of my youth in whom I could rejoice (Prov. 5:18). I knew what kind of character to seek and the values we had to share. I also realized I had to be actively looking (18:22) while, at the same time, preparing myself to be a godly husband. I had to grow in maturity and hold down a job to provide for a future family (1 Tim. 5:8). I needed strong convictions about church and ministry, children and marriage. I sought wise counsel while seeking this excellent wife who would be a helpmate to me and a loving mother to my children (Prov. 31:10-31). I now thank the Lord constantly for my wife and pray that my children will one day be equally blessed in marriage.

PRAYER: *Dear Heavenly Father, Thank you for the blessing of marriage and for my excellent wife. Help me to rejoice in her always as your gift to me. I pray for each of my children as they may one day choose a spouse of their own. Help them to marry wisely according to your will and to enjoy many years of happiness. In your Son's name, Amen.*

--------------□--------------

Write down one way you will apply today's Proverb:

22

DISCIPLE-MAKING

Train up a child in the way he should go;
even when he is old he will not depart from it.
- PROVERBS 22:6

One day, my son asked me why I still had children. It was an oddly-phrased question, so I asked him to explain: "What else would I do with my children?"

He suggested, "You could sell them."

I replied jokingly, "I don't think I could get very much for them."

So he insisted, "I think you could get $6 million for each child."

Some quick math: That's $24 million (much more than the cost to raise them). Unfortunately dads, we cannot sell our progeny, so it's time we learned to parent them. You are God's instrument in your children's lives to bring them into a relationship with him. As Moses exhorted the people of Israel:

> You shall love the LORD your God with all your heart and with all your soul and with all your might. And these words that I command you today shall be on your heart. You shall teach them diligently to your children, and shall talk of them when you sit in your house, and when you walk by the way, and when you lie down, and when you rise (Deut. 6:5-7).

Dads, you must train your children to love the Lord your God. Teach them the Word of God daily through instruction and example. Speak with them in the car and at the breakfast table. Model a biblical example from the moment they wake up until right before bedtime. Every moment, whether failure or success, is a parenting moment. Proverbs 22:6 declares, "Train up a child in the way he should go; even when he is old he will not depart from it." Now "to train up" is used elsewhere in Scripture for the dedication of important buildings or an important person like the high priest. This "dedication" not only points to an object's initial use, but also to the purpose for which it was set apart. "To train up a child" could therefore mean "to prepare a child for an intentional purpose from the moment he is born." As the twig is bent, so grows the tree.

Often I look at my boys and know exactly what their mischievous minds are thinking (because I was once their age): Should I dip my hand in the fish tank? Should I shove my brother off his chair? Should I listen to my mother or pretend I don't hear? I can see the difficult struggle between right and wrong as I seek to shepherd their hearts wisely.

Dads, do not surrender authority to your children by neglecting consistent biblical instruction and loving discipline (Eph. 6:4). Proverbs reminds us that every child is born a fool (22:15) and must learn wisdom in order to navigate this fallen world. Dads, you are God's gracious gift to your children whether they recognize it or not. So are you cultivating grace in your home by the way you live and teach?

Jesus exhorts us to view parenting as a means of intentionally fulfilling the Great Commission:

> And Jesus came and said to them, "All authority in heaven and on earth has been given to me. Go therefore and make disciples of all nations, baptizing them in the name of the Father and of the Son and of the Holy Spirit, teaching them to observe all that I have commanded you. And behold, I am with you always, to the end of the age" (Matt. 28:18-20).

Parenting is more than childcare—more than providing food to eat and a roof over their heads—more than video game consoles and a vacation once a year. Parenting is the hard work of discipleship. The skillful patience to be a godly father, however, comes just as naturally as obedience to a child. Dads, your unbelieving children are death-deserving sinners who need Jesus to become their Savior and Lord (Rom. 3:23-25). Jesus, with all the authority of heaven and earth, has commissioned you to make disciples of your children. So go to your children with the gospel, lead them to salvation, baptize them in union with the church, and teach them to obey everything Jesus commanded in his Word. Then trust that God is always with you as you make disciples in your family.

Dads, you must diligently train up your children. Think about it: You do potty training and training wheels. You train them to tie their shoes, to eat healthy food, and not to burp at the dinner table (when their mother is present). You spend the first twenty months training your children how to walk and talk and the next twenty years how to sit down and be quiet. Shouldn't you also train them to glorify God and to serve for the good of others (Matt. 22:37-39)? You have the wrong goal if parenting success simply means a good college and a good job and a good spouse and good morals, but no relationship with Jesus Christ. Dads, go make disciples of your children. Then teach them how to make disciples of others.

PRAYER: *Dear Heavenly Father, My children are a priceless treasure. I long for them to receive the best of life, but most importantly to receive the best of you. Teach me to train them every moment every day to seek a relationship with you. May they follow you while they are young and walk with you for eternity. In your Son's name, Amen.*

--------------□--------------

Write down one way you will apply today's Proverb:

23

LOVE

Better is a dinner of herbs where love is
than a fattened ox and hatred with it.
- PROVERBS 15:17

Raising children requires a foundation of love. As Hall-of-Fame baseball player Harmon Killebrew shared when, as a child, he destroyed the lawn fielding grounders with his dad. His mother commented on the trampled grass and his dad replied, "Honey, we're not raising grass here. We're raising boys." Similarly, "Better is a dinner of herbs where love is than a fattened ox and hatred with it" (15:17). Dads, even if your mouth waters over a really juicy steak, it is still better to chew on salad surrounded by a loving family. Your kids rarely need more stuff, but they do need your love. Labor to build a relationship with your children because all the money in the world can fill your house with things, but it cannot make a family.

Love your children with your time by remembering four basic words: Read. Pray. Work. Play. First, spend time reading God's Word in family devotions and personal discipleship. You don't need to be a scholar to read the Bible. In our family worship before bedtime, we try to read a ten-minute devotional and count any subsequent discussion as a victory. Don't get frustrated as children have the uncanny ability to listen even as they turn cartwheels.

Second, pray for your children and also pray with them. Show them by example your intimate parent-child relationship with God. In our family, we don't expect our children to pray like Puritans, but we do encourage them to pray simple prayers: "Thank God for one thing and ask him for one thing." We also try to model a relationship with God by praying about major decisions as a family.

Third, work alongside your children. Help them with tasks and projects they have been assigned for school and enlist them to help with household chores. Remind them that they are a contributing member of the household. Your patient instruction is well-worth the added effort and will teach them skills for a lifetime.

Fourth, don't forget to play. Explore what each child likes to do and spend quality time with them both individually and together. You don't even need to enjoy the activity yourself to enjoy being with them, although it helps to share common interests. Read, pray, work, play, and reach your child's heart.

Dads, love your children with your time and also with your words, for "death and life are in the power of the tongue" (18:21a). Words can either encourage or criticize; build up or tear down. Are your words gracious like honey (16:24) or do they break your child's spirit (15:4)? Your child must hear in your everyday speech that she is loved. Dads, this past week, what kind of power did you wield with words?

Finally, love your children by your example. You can tell but never teach, unless you practice what you preach. So live the way you want your child to become. Sadly Solomon, the writer of Proverbs, was a poor example to his son. Although the wisest man to ever live, he squandered the bulk of his life (see Eccl. 1). His son, Rehoboam, then followed his example instead of his instruction (1 Kgs. 12:1-19). Dads, there will be days when you are exhausted, pulling out your hair, and crying to Jesus because you do not know what else to do. You will find your children scribbling with permanent markers on the wall, yelling at you in rebellious anger, or telling lies about their grades in school. In that moment, you must make a choice. Do you address their sinful character with sinful character of your own or do you address their shortcomings with the love of Christ? If you see your role as discipling your child to become more like Jesus, then you will set a Christ-like example especially when addressing their sin. As J. C. Ryle writes in *The Duties of Parents*: "To give children good instruction, and a bad example, is the same as pointing out the way to heaven, while we take their hand and lead them down the road to hell."

It seems absurd that any father must be told to love his children. Yet how often do you choose your convenience over theirs? How often do you instruct behavior without caring for their souls? How often do you speak unkind words without asking their forgiveness? Dads, loving your children begins with knowing that you yourself are loved by God (1 John 4:19). Reaching their hearts begins with God first exposing yours. "So we have come to know and to believe the love that God has for us. God is love, and whoever abides in love abides in God, and God abides in him" (v. 16). God is the source of love. So when you love, your children see God in you. They will know you are a follower of Christ by your Christ-like love for them (John 13:34-35). Dads, your most loving role is to train your children to love Jesus with all their heart.

PRAYER: *Dear Heavenly Father, Help me to love my children well with my time, my words, and my example. Remind me in moments of parenting exhaustion that I am loved by you and have the unparalleled privilege of showing my children the love of Christ. Change my heart to help change theirs. In your Son's name, Amen.*

--------------□--------------

Write down one way you will apply today's Proverb:

—24—

OBEDIENCE

The fear of the LORD is the beginning of knowledge;
fools despise wisdom and instruction.
Hear, my son, your father's instruction,
and forsake not your mother's teaching.
- PROVERBS 1:7-8

When my son started second grade, I asked him what he had learned in school and his answer was intriguing. He said his teacher was instructing them how to be second graders.

Curious, I asked, "What does that mean?"

He replied with his chest puffed out: "In first grade we just had to listen, but in second grade we must also remember." Now that's a good lesson for all of us. We must not merely listen to God's Word, but also remember and obey (Jas. 1:22). Unfortunately, dads, your little rebels often find obedience to be difficult.

Late one evening I told my boys, "It's time to brush your teeth and go to bed." And one of them shouted, "No!" It was a reflex action. He didn't even pause to think about his answer, yet the very fact that I had issued a command was enough for him to rebel. I was ready to unleash all of my parenting wrath, but then something amazing happened. My son stopped, virtually in mid-air while jumping on the couch, and said to himself, "Oh, wait. Obedience means now." Then he went off to brush his teeth. I stood there speechless, not knowing whether to laugh or to cry. Even funnier, his brothers were grinning like Christmas had come early, because this was the first time after years of instruction and discipline that this particular son had shown any sign of comprehensive obedience. Now I know there's still a ton of parenting to do, yet that is the same story of slow sanctification in each of our lives. Christ-like obedience does not develop overnight.

Growing in character takes time and practice like learning how to ride a bike. When my boys first began, I held the bicycle seat and walked beside them as they wobbled down the street. Soon I was running behind them until finally I let go as they coasted on their own. At first, they were nervous about falling so I bundled them up in layers of clothing, but now they zip around with reckless abandon. And just like riding a bike, your children will never forget the patterns of discipline they cultivate in their youth.

Developing Christ-like character requires practice. If you and your wife are used to throwing around angry words, it may seem strange when one of you turns away wrath with a gentle answer (Prov. 15:1). If anxiety overwhelms you because of life's pressures, faith in God may feel like leaping over the edge of a cliff (3:5-6). If gossip entices you to go out of your way to hear it and out of your way to tell it, then backing off may feel like cutting out your tongue (11:13).

Developing Christ-like character feels awkward at first (and a little bit scary), yet habitual obedience eventually becomes like second nature. In our home, obedience means quickly, respectfully, and completely. We ask for obedience within the time allotted (e.g., Rom. 5:6; Gal. 4:4), with the right attitude (e.g., Luke 22:42; Jas. 1:2), and with full completion (e.g., Heb. 1:3; 10:12). This was the example of Jesus' obedience to his heavenly Father.

Many in Hawaii are familiar with the city life of Honolulu and the beaches of Waikiki, yet tourists rarely venture into the island center of Oahu —a mountainous rain forest where komodo dragons still roam in the caves and crevices. One day, my friend and I strapped on packs and explored the valley until we found a hiking trail heading up the mountain. Surrounded by luscious vegetation on all sides, the rain poured down so hard we could barely see. Yet as long as we followed the well-worn track we knew we could not get lost. In like manner, your children are hiking through the jungle of life without a clear vision of the peak. They might feel fearfully alone in the pouring rain and even hear the hissing of dragons.

Dads, teach your children to learn from wise teachers who have gone before them: "I have taught you the way of wisdom; I have led you in the paths of uprightness" (Prov. 4:11). "Paths" speak of well-worn tracks in the ground which did not come about because just one person walked that way. These are the well-worn tracks of godly saints who trod the ancient paths before us (Heb. 12:1). Your children will learn obedience not only by studying God's Word, but also by walking in the steps of faithful theologians, pastors, and parents. It is prideful folly to start from scratch when the trail has already been blazed. According to Proverbs, as long as you can see the well-worn track, you are doing alright. The paths of uprightness reveal that other Christians have walked this way before. Wise children listen to wise parents.

PRAYER: *Dear Heavenly Father, Help me to grow in wisdom as a parent. Teach me to walk in the paths of righteousness as I study your Word and learn from those who have gone before me. Show me how to pass on these truths to my children and lead them in the way of obedience. In your Son's name, Amen.*

-------------□-------------

Write down one way you will apply today's Proverb:

—25—

TRUTH

Every word of God proves true;
he is a shield to those who take refuge in him.
- PROVERBS 30:5

One day, I came home and asked my boys what they did all day.

They replied, "We were making money."

Proud of their entrepreneurial spirit, I asked, "Did you start a business? Were you selling something?"

"No," they corrected me, "We were *making* money." Apparently, there was a tiny counterfeit operation going on in my house.

So I said to them, "You realize your currency is worth nothing if there's no bank to back it." Likewise, dads, your child's faith is worthless unless it is grounded in the truth of God's Word.

"Train up a child in the way he should go" (Prov. 22:6a) literally means, "Train up a child upon the mouth of his way." "Upon the mouth" or "from the lips" was a Hebrew idiom meaning, "according to," or, "in accord with," like a servant waiting eagerly at the beck and call of his master. Dads, you must train your children to live according to the way of the Lord. The word "way" occurs nearly seventy times in Proverbs to describe the habitual choices and direction one takes in life. Picture trudging back-and-forth through a field of grass until you have carved a well-worn path. So also, you must habitually walk in the way of the Lord until it becomes a trail.

Dads, instruct your children by example. Tread the path of wisdom and righteousness instead of folly and sin. Walk in God's way, then train your children to follow. Instruction happens not only when your children are in trouble, but also at the breakfast table, on the way to school, and during bedtime prayers. Continually shepherd their hearts in the way of God's wisdom, for the child "who walks with the wise grows wise" (13:20a). More than a lecture, this requires the witness of a life well-lived. Your righteous character will bless your children as they learn with you to love the Word of

God: “The righteous who walks in his integrity—blessed are his children after him! (20:7). So how’s your prayer life? How’s your devotional life and your walk with the Lord? Choose to cultivate your relationship with God and the benefits will overflow to your children.

Instruct by example and also with creativity like Jesus who said, “Look at the birds of the air,” and, “Consider the lilies of the field” (see Matt. 6:25-34). In Proverbs, the ant instructs the jobless sluggard (6:6-11) and the loaf of bread instructs young men hooked on porn (v. 26). The gold ring in the pig’s snout instructs the teen who wears her theology on designer jeans and a bare midriff (11:22). So dads, be creative when teaching God’s Word, but also find help in the creativity of others. My boys often chatter with excitement about their Sunday School adventures: eating a meal in Abraham’s tent, fighting a battle with the Assyrians, or walking on water with Jesus. Our children also love radio drama like *Adventures in Odyssey*, Bible stories on video, and play-acting passages from Scripture. Creativity brings biblical truth to life so that your children will remember.

Third, instruct your children in community with the help of your church family. A good church will help your children pray, memorize Bible verses, sing praise songs, learn about Jesus, and engage in discipleship. Certainly, God places the ultimate responsibility on parents (Exod. 13:8; Deut. 4:9-10; 6:4-25), but the church can offer much assistance. Dads, join a church with gospel-centered ministries for children and youth. God’s family should offer counseling and mentorship to cultivate health in your family. Take advantage of the resources which support your role as parents. Don’t let academics, athletics, social engagements, or laziness keep you from the loving fellowship of the church.

Finally, instruct children not only in the whole counsel of Scripture, but specifically in the gospel truth. Teach them that God is the loving Ruler and Creator of the world (Prov. 3:19). Direct your children to observe the beauty and the power of God’s creation (Ps. 19:1-6). Teach them that God is holy as you explain rules like speed limits and bedtime curfews. Remind them that “the eyes of the LORD are in every place, keeping watch on the evil and the good” (Prov. 15:3). Weep over the sin of man as you point out the consequences of sin and death around us. For example, sin is revealed in the impatience of a traffic jam or the trauma of a playground fistfight. Death is in the newspaper, at grandpa’s funeral, and a goldfish swirling down the toilet bowl. It is the story of Adam and Eve and every story after. Warn your children about the consequences of their own personal sin, for a fool's disobedience brings "sorrow to his mother" (10:1b; 15:20b; 17:21). "A foolish son is a grief to his father and bitterness to her who bore him" (17:25). "A foolish son is ruin to his father" (19:13a) and a source of shame (28:7b). The consequence of his sin is spiritual death (Rom. 6:23a).

Most importantly, reveal the truth to your children that Christ is Savior. Tell them the story of the cross in a thousand different ways until it seeps into the way they understand the world and understand themselves. Point out evidences of grace in their life and in the lives of others who are drawing them to Jesus. Help them see how their miniature story of creation, fall, redemption, and consummation finds its place in God's bigger story. Then teach them to repent of sin and believe in Christ.

Dads, you will have no greater joy than leading your children to the Lord and bringing them up in discipleship. This is successful parenting: To dedicate your children to the Lord, then teaching, training, and guiding them on the path that they must walk. Even if he becomes a famous doctor or a wealthy businessman—even if she wins the Nobel Prize or the Pulitzer, all that is icing on the cake. So may we claim with John: "I have no greater joy than to hear that my children are walking in the truth" (3 John 4).

PRAYER: *Dear Heavenly Father, I pray for strength to instruct my children how to walk in the truth. Remind me to instill in them a love for the gospel and a love for Christ, their Savior. Help me point out evidences of your grace which direct their hearts to you. In your Son's name, Amen.*

-------------□-------------

Write down one way you will apply today's Proverb:

26

FAITH

The father of the righteous will greatly rejoice;
he who fathers a wise son will be glad in him.
Let your father and mother be glad; let her who bore you rejoice.
My son, give me your heart, and let your eyes observe my ways.
\- PROVERBS 23:24-26

Dads, train your children to put their faith in God. One day I was sitting on our living room step, silently confessing my spiritual weaknesses, when my son came down from his nap. He sat next to me and we prayed together for a bit. Then after a few moments, he asked, "Daddy, why are you sitting on the step?" (He associated sitting on the step with having a time-out). I told him that I was praying for our family. Yet as I made that incredibly pious statement, I thought about all the times my boys had seen me watching sports, typing on the computer, or reading a book. This was the first time any of them had ever "caught" me in prayer. Now, of course, I do not pray to show off for my children, but I certainly do not pray enough. Praying regularly with your children trains them to put their faith in God. Praying regularly for your children trains you.

Dads, rely on God's Holy Spirit (Eph. 5:18b) who will empower you to lead your children "in the discipline and instruction of the Lord" (6:4). "The father of the righteous will greatly rejoice; he who fathers a wise son will be glad in him" (Prov. 23:24). Here is biblical hope for countless parents who face the challenges and confusion of child-rearing: "Keep on going! It's worth it! Have faith that God's way is the right way." For the Proverbs are not a sledgehammer of guilt, but an encouragement to hope. So "trust in the Lord with all your heart" (3:5a), then trust him with your child's heart.

"Let your father and mother be glad; let her who bore you rejoice. My son, give me your heart, and let your eyes observe my ways" (23:25-26). Note carefully that this proverb does not say, "My son, give me your behavior," as if outward change was most important. Nor does it say, "My son, give me your physical presence," as if all that matters is placing a child in the right place at the right time: "Get them to church and a Christian school, so they'll turn out all right." No, verse 26 clearly states, "My son, give me your heart." So also, "My son, if your heart is wise, my heart too will be glad" (v. 15; see 27:11). A godly father is like the diligent farmer who sows in faith. The farmer plants when the field is bare and the seed is small because he envisions the future harvest. So also, the wise father faithfully parents according to biblical principles. Parenting is a life of faith, so trust in the Lord and not yourself.

Dads, beware of acquiring an ownership mentality: "These are my children. They belong to me, so I can train them whichever way I want." Do not forget your parenting goal to make disciples and lead your children in a Godward direction. You are merely a divine instrument to point your children to God's glorious story and the grace of his redemption. In your weakness, God alone receives the glory (1 Cor. 1:31). For the God who first transformed you did not call you to this task of parenthood because you were able, but because you were unable. He parents you as you parent your children. He exposes your daily need for grace and reveals how your story of creation, fall, redemption, and consummation finds its place in his greater story. God will never call you to a task without giving you everything you need to do it and he never sends you into the fray without also going with you.

At times, you may forget your identity in Christ and seek to find it in your children. You may worship your children by sacrificing all your time and money, thoughts and desires at the altar of your family. Yet realize that children make terrible idols, for they are lost and rebellious, foolish and blind. They will chew you up and spit you out if you prop them up as idols to do your bidding. They will always disappoint, for they are self-ruling sinners who do not care about serving you. So dads, root out your own selfish desires before you root out theirs. Come before the Lord, confessing moments you have made your children into idols. Seek God's grace to train up your children in love, obedience, and truth. Then trust the Lord to transform their hearts to be like his. "Trust in the Lord with all your heart" and with your children's hearts.

PRAYER: *Dear Heavenly Father, Guard my heart from making my children* *into idols for my own satisfaction. Show me how to raise them in the Lord and not to please my pride. Strengthen my faith in you as a testimony to your goodness that will lead my children to personal faith as well. In your Son's name, Amen.*

-------------□-------------

Write down one way you will apply today's Proverb:

——————27——————

DISCIPLINE

Whoever spares the rod hates his son,
but he who loves him is diligent to discipline him.
- PROVERBS 13:24

"Train up a child in the way he should go" (Prov. 22:6a) means, "Don't let your child do whatever he wants." For Proverbs teaches that discipline is both necessary and good: "Whoever spares the rod hates his son, but he who loves him is diligent to discipline him" (13:24). "Discipline your son, for there is hope; do not set your heart on putting him to death" (19:18; see 23:13-14).

Dads, consider three simple words for the practice of discipline: teach, warn, and enforce. For example, when training your child not to run across the street, first teach appropriate behavior: "Son, please hold Daddy's hand as we walk across the street." Second, warn against the consequences: "See all those cars rushing by. You could be squashed like a little frog if you run across the street by yourself." Then if he disobeys, enforce with discipline: "Son, you did not listen to Daddy when you ran into the street without holding my hand. That was disobedient and dangerous. And because I love you, I must now remind you with discipline." Teach, warn, enforce. Put most of your effort into the first two and you will need much less of the third.

Consider also three simple words for the manner of discipline: redemptive, appropriate, and consistent. First, discipline your children redemptively. Train them to obey, though it may cost you trouble and tears. Teach them that it's not their way, right away and do not appease them for the sake of efficiency. Keep them at the table if they refuse to eat their vegetables and patiently rebuke them for throwing a tantrum. Most children do not wake up thinking, "How can I frustrate and manipulate my parents today? How can I rebel against their authority?" Yet although children are not intentionally evil, they are born with a bent (Ps. 51:5; Prov. 22:15; Rom. 5:12). Like Adam and Eve, they want to see, touch, and taste the forbidden fruit the moment your back is turned (Gen. 3:6). Would you, however, tolerate such conduct from a coworker? What if your spouse threw a tantrum or your neighbor demanded to always get his way? You wouldn't stand for that, so why let your children slide with foolish words and rebellious behavior? You will not tolerate their sin if your goal is to train them up in godliness because redemptive discipline gently confronts (Gal. 6:1). It is not you against your children, but you with them against their sin. You are on a rescue mission to save your children from themselves, for their obedience to you will train them in obedience to Christ.

Second, discipline appropriately by remembering that every child (even in the same family) is unique. They each have different levels of maturity and respond better to different forms of discipline. Some need "the board of education applied to the seat of learning" and some need only a glance to melt their hearts. The type of clay determines the vessel. Some clay is elastic and supple, while other clay is crumbly and hard to shape. So also, every child must be handled with the discernment of a skillful potter. Realize also that Proverbs describes different levels of training appropriate to the situation, for God gives parents both the rod and reproof (Prov. 29:15). The rod includes any kind of discipline: time-outs, removal of privilege, additional work, wisely-administered spankings, and natural consequences. Whereas reproof includes any kind of verbal instruction: encouragement, warning, teaching Scripture, and appealing to conscience. Parents must be skilled with both rod and reproof.

Finally, discipline must be consistent, for sneaky sinners will always find the weakest link. If momma says, "No ice cream," they'll go find dad. You and your spouse, however, are a parenting team, so form a united front. Never contradict each other in front of the children or allow them to play one parent against the other. As we say in our family, "Mommy and Daddy are one." Also be consistent in how you administer discipline: "Let your yes be yes and your no be no" (Matt. 5:37). Erratic parenting is a form of deception which will provoke your children to anger (Eph. 6:4a). Do not overlook an offense three times, but on the fourth time discipline severely. The discipline process should be so predictable that your children can anticipate the discernible pattern. For example, after praying together, ask good questions which lead them to confession: "What did daddy tell you to do? Did you listen? What did you want more than wanting to obey?" Then after you administer the discipline, express your love for them both physically and verbally. Your discipline should be so consistent that your children will know what you are about to say and do before it happens.

Discipline redemptively, appropriately, and consistently, then always bathe it with gentle affirmation and an encouragement to embrace the gospel. The ultimate purpose of discipline is to cultivate Christ-empowered righteousness (Prov. 20:11). Discipline must soften your child's heart to become a receptive follower of Jesus Christ just as your heavenly Father does for you: "My son, do not despise the LORD's discipline or be weary of his reproof, for the LORD reproves him whom he loves, as a father the son in whom he delights" (3:11-12; see Heb. 12:6).

PRAYER: *Dear Heavenly Father, Thank you for disciplining me when I go astray. Even in the pain, I am reminded that you love me and assured that I am your child. Thank you for sending your Son to bear the ultimate brunt of your wrath upon the cross. Teach me to lead my children into a right relationship with you. Show me how to discipline wisely, appropriately, and consistently in a way that leads them to redemption. In your Son's name, Amen.*

--------------□--------------

Write down one way you will apply today's Proverb:

28

SHEPHERDING

My son, keep your father's commandment,
and forsake not your mother's teaching.
Bind them on your heart always; tie them around your neck.
When you walk, they will lead you;
when you lie down, they will watch over you;
and when you awake, they will talk with you.
For the commandment is a lamp and the teaching a light,
and the reproofs of discipline are the way of life.

\- PROVERBS 6:20-23

Dads, shepherd your children as their protector and provider. Like the Good Shepherd, lay down your life for them (John 10:11). Consider one simple shepherding practice which has yielded some of my favorite parenting memories. Schedule to meet with each of your children once a week on a designated day. My children call it their special time with daddy. You can do anything you want during this time: wrestle, have pillow fights, eat ice cream, watch football, play a game, or read a book. You can ask about their day or what they learned in Sunday School that week. Sometimes when I'm tired, I just close my eyes and let them talk about whatever they want to talk about (which usually ends up being sports or Star Wars). Occasionally, you can introduce spiritual conversations or pray with them. Perhaps read a theology book for kids and invite their questions. During our special time, we often discuss the Scripture passage our church will study on the upcoming Sunday. Then as we read it together, they always have questions.

Dads, never be afraid of questions. It's perfectly fine to say, "That's a great question," or, "Let's study it together," or, "Why don't we ask for help." My children often ask questions that no adult has ever asked in all my years of ministry and I simply have to answer, "I don't know."

For example, after reading John 10 together, I asked my son, "Why do you think the Bible describes people as sheep?" We talked about all the silly things that sheep do which are like all the silly things that people do. Then as we discussed the difference between good shepherds and hired hands (vv. 12-13), my son asked, "Do the hired hands lose all their money if they run away and leave the sheep behind?"

I replied with my own question (since I didn't have an answer): "Would you rather have money or your life?" He did not respond as quickly as I would have liked, yet pondering that question cemented for him how Jesus stood in the way of danger to care for us.

My son then asked, "So who are the thieves and the robbers?"

I replied, "They are the people who try to harm the sheep."

"Oh, you mean, like the Pharisees."

"Yes, exactly the Pharisees."

Then I asked, "So what do you think Jesus meant when he said the good shepherd lays down his life for the sheep?"

"Oh, he's talking about his death. He's about to die on the cross."

"That's right. Jesus' death on the cross demonstrates how much he loves us and his rising from the dead shows how powerful he is to save us." We discussed what makes us afraid and how Jesus brings comfort.

Then finally, I asked, "Now why did some people say Jesus was crazy or demon-possessed?"

My son answered, "Because Jesus taught a lot of things."

"That's right. Jesus made many claims that would have sounded crazy unless they were true." I could see the light bulb turn on: Whether or not Jesus spoke the truth made the difference between whether he was crazy and whether he was Lord.

All I did was ask good questions since my role is not to save my kids, but to lead them to Jesus. So also, dads, when you read the Bible with your children, teach them to listen to the shepherd's voice (vv. 3-5). Show them that Jesus is the only door to a personal relationship with God (vv. 7, 9). By doing so, you open their hearts to the good news that Jesus died to forgive sinners and rose from the dead to bring us into his flock.

Scripture must inform your shepherding strategy like Solomon, who pairs parental teaching with the law of God (see Prov. 6:20-23): "Son, listen to me. My authority comes not just from being your father, but from the Word of God. And do not merely listen, but bind these words to your heart. Hide them in your soul. Memorize them. Treasure them. Keep them always with you. Then as you walk through life, they will lead you like a shepherd. They will teach you to discern wise decisions, protect you in times of fear, and comfort you in suffering. They will give you peace when you sleep and guidance when you wake. My son, God himself will speak to you in his Word. When you actively engage with Scripture, you will have lively conversations with your Creator. These words are not dead letters on a page, but alive! I entrust to you, my son, a precious lamp to light your way when the trail grows dark and have designed my loving discipline to keep you on the path of life. Son, listen to me as I teach you God's Word."

Dads, I encourage you to dedicate special time for your children. Start by spending ten minutes a week per child and schedule it in like all your other appointments. Shepherd your children like Jesus shepherds you.

PRAYER: *Dear Heavenly Father, Thank you for sending your Son to be my Good Shepherd. Teach me to listen to his voice and take comfort in his presence. Show me how to lovingly shepherd my children until they can follow the voice of Jesus on their own. Strengthen me to daily lay down my interests for theirs and to be your instrument in their lives. In your Son's name, Amen.*

-------------□-------------

Write down one way you will apply today's Proverb:

29

SURRENDER

The heart of man plans his way,
but the LORD establishes his steps.
- PROVERBS 16:9

"Magic sand," he said with mystery as he climbed into the minivan. His brother looked at him curiously, so he explained: "I have magic sand and if I put it in my pocket, it will turn into money. He then proceeded to theatrically produce a brand new five-dollar bill.

"Where'd you get that?" his brother asked.

"Magic sand," was the reply.

At home, we finally coaxed it from our son that a friend at school had given him five dollars for helping him do his homework. He knew in his budding conscience that it was wrong to take the money, so he conjured up a creative explanation to justify its existence: magic sand. Initially, we thought about making him return the money, but then we prayerfully left the decision up to him. For despite our steadfast denials, children grow up quickly and cannot always be told the right thing to do in every situation. Five dollars seemed a relatively tiny step toward personal responsibility. Thankfully, our son decided to return the money (or donate to charity if his friend refused to take it), yet this lesson taught us to surrender our children to God.

Dads, as you steward your children, you must constantly surrender your parenting to the Lord. If you have chosen to follow Jesus, then you must give him your family: the way you raise your kids, love your spouse, and depend on God's plan for your future. Surrender, however, will grate against your idol of control. When our family would play MarioKart together, one of our sons would press the gas while my wife steered the kart. But as will happen in a video game, they would sometimes careen off a cliff or crash into a wall. At those times, my then 5-year old son would shout in frustration: "Mommy! Drive straight!" We had to calm him down with time-outs until he remembered they were both on the same team. Sadly, however, we do that to

Jesus all the time. We hand him the steering wheel to let him drive, but insist on navigating. We tell Jesus which way we think he should go and instruct him to speed up or slow down: "Watch out for that curve! Pass up that slowpoke!" We get so mad when Jesus does not do exactly what we want that he must give us spiritual time-outs to address our idolatrous demand for control.

Dads, learn to surrender your family to Jesus. Instead of clinging to power and control, let him fully take the wheel. The Lord's providence will change your course and draw you back. According to Proverbs 16:9, "The heart of man plans his way, but the LORD establishes his steps" (19:21; 20:24). One vacation, our family planned a road trip, booked hotels, and saved up money. But on the day before we left, God allowed a tiny little rock to fly through a tiny little opening in the grill of our van to put it completely out of commission. So we ended up shortening our road trip, but that's not all. While on vacation, our son needed emergency surgery (Yes, another ambulance ride!). Yet because God had providentially changed our itinerary, we were in the right city with the best specialist who could provide optimal treatment for our son. Dads, it is never wrong to make plans. In fact, it's wise. But do not worry when your best-laid plans often go awry, for the sovereign God will determine your way and wisely establish your steps.

PRAYER: *Dear Heavenly Father, You are the Ruler and Lord of my life, so let me trust your sovereign authority to correct my course when I stray. Help me submit to your leading as I steward my family for your good purposes. Let my surrender be an example of faith to them, so that they will follow you in faith themselves. In your Son's name, Amen.*

--------------□--------------

Write down one way you will apply today's Proverb:

30

PURPOSE

Where there is no prophetic vision the people cast off restraint, but blessed is he who keeps the law.

- PROVERBS 29:18

Belly buttons were the subject of our dinner conversation as I asked, "How are babies attached to their mommies?"

One of our sons, eager to express his newfound knowledge, shouted out: "With an extension cord!"

Now I suppose the umbilical can be a kind of extension cord, yet consider that our belly button now serves no productive purpose except to remind us we were at one time completely dependent on the nourishment of another. I used this to teach my boys that, spiritually speaking, we are completely dependent on the sustaining power of the Almighty God: "He is before all things, and in him all things hold together" (Col. 1:17; see Heb. 1:3a). Dads, whether you are contemplating your wrinkly navel or the stars in the sky or the beauties of nature, realize that all of creation declares the glory of God (Ps. 19:1). Worship the Lord for making it and worship him for sustaining it, for you have been created to glorify him.

Life is a journey, so put feet to your theology. Let doctrine impact the way you walk, live, and practice your faith. Then what you believe about God will transform the way you live your life. If you plan to travel from one city to another, you must take the proper highway. So also, if you are destined to spend eternity with Jesus, you will worship him with your life on earth. Your destination determines the path you take and your joy in the journey. For this reason, Solomon uses traveling imagery: "I have taught you the way of wisdom; I have led you in the paths of uprightness. When you walk, your step will not be hampered, and if you run, you will not stumble" (Prov. 4:11-12). If you want to be godly, then walk in God's Word. If you desire to be righteous, then study God's character. If you would make good decisions, then learn from God's wisdom. Study the map before heading out and at every fork along the way. Establish the step-by-step rhythm of spiritual disciplines "and if you run, you will not stumble." You won't grow weary (Isa. 5:27; 40:30-31) and you will not fall (Ps. 27:2; Jer. 50:32).

Dads, life is a series of forks in the road where decisions must be made, so pay attention! Don't miss the turn! There are only two ways to go. To the right is Wisdom Lane (Prov. 4:10-13), a narrow, but well-worn path which climbs a difficult hill. And to the left is Folly Freeway (vv. 14-17), an eight-lane expressway plunging downward with no apparent obstacles or traffic lights to slow you down. Which way do you plan to go? Success requires having the right goal and the means to achieve it: "Where there is no prophetic vision the people cast off restraint, but blessed is he who keeps the law" (29:18).

Dads, what goals have you established for your family? Our Sugimura family mission statement consists of five biblical principles to define our purpose for the journey.

1. *Worship the Lord*: "You shall love the Lord your God with all your heart and with all your soul and with all your mind. This is the great and first commandment" (Matt. 22:37-38).
2. *Cherish our family*: "Love is patient and kind; love does not envy or boast; it is not arrogant or rude. It does not insist on its own way; it is not irritable or resentful; it does not rejoice at wrongdoing, but rejoices with the truth. Love bears all things, believes all things, hopes all things, endures all things. Love never ends" (1 Cor. 13:4-8a).
3. *Edify the church*: "Go therefore and make disciples of all nations, baptizing them in the name of the Father and of the Son and of the Holy Spirit, teaching them to observe all that I have commanded you. And behold, I am with you always, to the end of the age" (Matt. 28:19-20).
4. *Fulfill your gifting*: "As each has received a gift, use it to serve one another, as good stewards of God's varied grace . . . in order that in everything God may be glorified through Jesus Christ" (1 Pet. 4:10, 11b).
5. *Bless our community*: "You shall love your neighbor as yourself" (Matt. 22:39).

We often discuss each principle as we live life together as a family. For example, before hosting a party in our home we might brainstorm about blessing our community. Before serving together, we might discuss how to fulfill our gifting and edify the church. Perhaps our most frequent reminder is to cherish our family, but our foundational principle is to worship the Lord. Dads, I challenge you to take time this week to develop your own family's mission statement.

PRAYER: *Dear Heavenly Father, We desire to be a family who serves together with an eternal purpose. Teach us to worship you with our lives, to cherish our family in every situation, and to fulfill our gifting as we edify the church. Help us to be a testimony of grace as we bless our community and lead them to a knowledge of you. In your Son's name, Amen.*

-------------□-------------

Write down one way you will apply today's Proverb:

31

TREASURE

My son, if you receive my words and
treasure up my commandments with you,
making your ear attentive to wisdom and
inclining your heart to understanding;
yes, if you call out for insight and raise your voice for understanding,
if you seek it like silver and search for it as for hidden treasures,
then you will understand the fear of the LORD and
find the knowledge of God.
- PROVERBS 2:1-5

My son, when learning how to read, occasionally came across a word he had never seen before. He would spot the first few letters and take a guess at the rest of the word. If he got it wrong, then he would take another guess and then another. I would gently correct him: "No, son, try to sound out every word. Don't get lazy. You can do this." There were times, of course, when the word was just too difficult and I had to tell him the answer. I knew, however, that he would never learn to read by guessing, but by good old-fashioned hard work. Likewise, our heavenly Father makes us study diligently to ingrain the truths of Scripture. Although wisdom is a gift of God, wisdom requires work. Thus Proverbs 2 promotes this active learning: "Receive my words," "treasure up my commandments," "[make] your ear attentive," "[incline] your heart," "call out," "raise your voice," "seek . . . and search," "understand . . . and find."

Dads, you must daily excavate God's Word: "Seek it like silver and search for it as for hidden treasures" (Prov. 2:4). Digging is hard, but it yields great wealth. For example, what would you do if, in your backyard, buried six feet below the ground, was a massive cache of diamonds? Would you yawn and return to surfing the web? Would you plop on the couch to watch a reality show about treasure hunters? Or would you round up digging tools and get to work?

By analogy, is your Bible a mine or a museum? Do you go to work every day in God's Word? Do you strap on your hard hat and your headlamp? Do you bring the right tools and the motivation to search for buried treasure? Do you turn over every rock and verse, combing through debris, determined not to miss a precious gem? Or is your Bible like a museum displaying dusty artifacts from expeditions past? Maybe someone else found them first and you are just the curator? You might visit the museum every Sunday or even work there. You might know the descriptive captions by heart, but you have never examined that treasure personally. Do not think yourself a treasure hunter unless you have labored in the mine. Even greedy men will rush after fools' gold and injure others to get it (1:10-19). How much more should be your single-minded fervency for the precious Word of God?

Dads, "if you bring your digging tools" (2:1-4), "then you will understand" (vv. 5-9) and be able to teach it to your children. Let God's Word rule your heart (Col. 3:16). Read, study, and think about its meaning. Examine the Scriptures even when taught by respected Bible teachers (e.g., Acts 17:11). Follow accepted rules of interpretation, instead of arbitrarily deciding what you feel the text should mean (2 Tim. 2:15). Shape your life to fit the Word of God and not God's Word to fit your life (Rom. 12:2). Then as you minister to your children, let God's Word be the basis of your instruction. God created your children to trust you from a young age, so do not neglect to teach them the whole counsel of God's Word (see Acts 20:27).

Lastly, speak this truth in love (Eph. 4:15). One day, my son and I were talking in the car about the armor of God. He was especially interested in "the sword of the Spirit, which is the Word of God" (Eph. 6:17b) and he asked if we smacked people on the head with it. I told him, "No, we just read it and explain it and let God do the rest" (Isa. 55:10-11).

PRAYER: *Dear Heavenly Father, Fill my heart with your Word that I may pass it on to my children. Help me search for it like buried treasure and delight in each discovery. Show me how to apply this joy as I lead my family on a treasure hunt through Scripture. In your Son's name, Amen.*

--------------□--------------

Write down one way you will apply today's Proverb:

Write down one way you will apply today's Proverb:

—32—

FRIENDSHIP

Whoever walks with the wise becomes wise,
but the companion of fools will suffer harm.
- PROVERBS 13:20

In kindergarten, one of my sons made a new friend named Chon-Chon. "That's an interesting name," I commented, "Is that a nickname? Is he ethnic?"

My son answered innocently, "I don't know," and proceeded to share about all the games he played with Chon-Chon. Every day, he would bring home a new story: "Chon-Chon said this. Chon-Chon did that."

These tales went on for several weeks until we finally learned from the school that there was no child enrolled by the name of Chon-Chon. My son had invented an imaginary friend. Now certainly good friends are hard to find, yet not so impossible that your children must make them up.

Proverbs exhorts you to find friends who will help you avoid folly (Prov. 18:1) and lovingly confront you with the truth: "Better is open rebuke than hidden love. Faithful are the wounds of a friend; profuse are the kisses of an enemy" (27:5-6; Eph. 4:25). Good friends strengthen you when you are anxious (Prov. 12:25) and speak words of healing (12:18b; 18:12a). They witness your intimate struggles, but keep your confidence (11:13) as they minister godly counsel: "The purpose in a man's heart is like deep water, but a man of understanding will draw it out" (20:5; Rom. 15:14). They know you and they know God's Word, then they bring the two together: "Oil and perfume make the heart glad, and the sweetness of a friend comes from his earnest counsel" (Prov. 27:9). Good friends help you better worship the God in whose image you were made (Gen. 1:27). They sharpen you like iron (Prov. 27:17) and compel you to love Christ more. A good friend will never abandon you (17:17), but will always seek your good: "A man of many companions may come to ruin, but there is a friend who sticks closer than a brother" (18:24). Thus it is better to cultivate a few good friendships, than to collect a multitude of shallow ones (13:20).

Dads, counsel your children to choose friends wisely, but also to forgive offenses and to seek forgiveness (Col. 3:13). Even good friends can sometimes be selfish or mean, insensitive or rude. At other times, your child may be the unfaithful one. He may use others for personal gain instead of loving them well (Prov. 6:12-14). She may speak unkindly about her peers (10:18). For this reason, God sent his Son to live a perfect life and to die a sacrificial death for sinners. Through Christ, your sinful child can be forgiven and brought into right relationship with God (1 John 1:3). As Jesus himself declared, “Greater love has no one than this, that someone lay down his life for his friends. You are my friends if you do what I command you” (John 15:13). Jesus calls us friends, though at one time we hated him and wanted nothing to do with him (Rom. 5:10). Dads, teach this gospel of friendship to your children, so that they become faithful friends who model Christ’s love.

PRAYER: *Dear Heavenly Father, Forgive me for the times when I have not been a faithful friend and remind me of your grace and mercy in my own life. Help me to guide my children to wisely choose their friends and to navigate the complex challenges of social interaction. May they be good friends to others by modeling the friendship of Christ. In your Son's name, Amen.*

--------------□--------------

Write down one way you will apply today's Proverb:

KINDNESS

Whoever pursues righteousness and kindness will find life, righteousness, and honor.
- PROVERBS 21:21

One evening, my wife and I played a game with our boys creatively called, "I like you because…" We put everyone's name into a hat and each took turns pulling one out. For each name we drew, we would give one reason why we liked that person. To our pleasant surprise, the boys loved this game. It took awhile, of course, to define the nature of a genuine compliment, but soon they began to enjoy both giving and receiving words of kindness. There were quite a few silly ones such as, "I like you because you are good at football," and, "I like you because you are smelly." But my favorite was when one of our boys looked deep into his mother's eyes and said, "Mommy, I like you because you are thoughtful and caring and hard-working." Our boys were so intent on the game that we played three rounds that first night and they were still handing out compliments during breakfast the next morning.

We must all practice being kind. So dads, I encourage you to try out this game with your own family. Don't be thrown off by the hilarity which ensues when a person selects his own name, but do take the time to define and demonstrate the nature of a true compliment. Most importantly, be ready to share your own words of kindness for each member in the family.

Dads, remind your children to be kind, but also that kindness is more than simply being nice to people who are nice to them. As Jesus commands, "Love your enemies and pray for those who persecute you" (Matt. 5:44). Or in the words of my boys, "Kindness is loving others even when they do things that you don't like. Kindness is responding with gentleness when someone takes your toy (Prov. 15:1). Kindness is bearing patiently with that annoying girl at school (1 Cor. 13:4a). Kindness is letting your brother choose the first dessert (v. 5) or deciding to forgive an offense (Eph. 4:32)." Dads, teach your children that kindness is hard, so that they will see their need for Jesus. They will often fail at kindness, whereas Jesus never did (Heb. 4:15). He was always kind, even to Judas who betrayed him (Luke 22:47-48) and to sinners like us for whom he died (Rom. 5:8). Your children need Jesus to forgive their lack of kindness and to declare them righteous before God. They need Jesus because kindness is only possible by the fruit of God's Holy Spirit (Gal. 5:22-23). They need Jesus who did not die to make them nice, but to make them new (2 Cor. 5:17).

Dads, remember also that you show kindness to your children by your example. Your little ones may frustrate you, pester you, grieve you, and anger you: "We're all going to enjoy this vacation if it kills us!" At such times, remember the love of Christ and "be kind to one another, tenderhearted, forgiving one another, as God in Christ forgave you" (Eph. 4:32). Your children are wicked reprobates in need of salvation who will fight and claw to get what they want from you. They often sin despite your best efforts to bring them up "in the discipline and instruction of the Lord" (6:4). Therefore, you must often forgive them "as God in Christ forgave you." Know, however, that "whoever pursues righteousness and kindness will find life, righteousness, and honor" (Prov. 21:21). Live God's way and he will bless you with the good life, the righteousness you seek, and the honor he only bestows upon his own. God alone can give you the strength to be a loving father who leads his children in the way of blessing (4:10-12). God alone rewards your kindness to your children with his lovingkindness toward you (3:1-12).

PRAYER: *Dear Heavenly Father, Help me to be tenderhearted toward my children even when I do not want to be kind. Remind me of your lovingkindness toward me and convict me of my shortcomings. Cultivate in me a love for Christ which compels me to be gracious and teach me the skillful wisdom of expressing kindness to those around me. In your Son's name, Amen.*

--------------□--------------

Write down one way you will apply today's Proverb:

34

LEGACY

How much better to get wisdom than gold!
To get understanding is to be chosen rather than silver.
- PROVERBS 16:16

I was named in honor of my grandfather who died a few weeks before I was born. His best friend persuaded my mother to call me, Tom, the name by which her father was known. I never met my grandfather in person, but I hear he was a character. He told fascinating tales of being a runaway slave in China, stowing aboard a ship to America, and traveling to Alaska as a cook with the U. S. army. He tricked my grandma into marrying him and worked hard to provide a better life. He loved his family, loved to joke around with friends, and one day learned to love the Lord. I never knew my grandfather, but I received his name.

Thankfully, my own children have been blessed to know all of their grandparents not just in the memories of others, but also in person. They are able to experience life together, eat meals, read books, play games, and celebrate birthdays. Our parents have been able to pass on a portion of their lives to a third generation. Most importantly, my father and mother were both the first to become Christians in their respective families. My parents then passed on their faith to me and I am passing it on to my children.

In the church, we also joyfully pass on our faith to successive generations, for children learn much from those who have gone before. As Paul exhorts Timothy, "And what you have heard from me in the presence of many witnesses entrust to faithful men who will be able to teach others also" (2 Tim. 2:2)—at least four generations of disciples who make disciples. We reinforce this generational upbringing in the church by calling every member to minister to children through Sunday school, youth ministry, Vacation Bible School, intercessory prayer, or simply demonstrating Christ-like love within the bounds of the believing family. It takes a whole church to make disciples of our children.

Proverbs 4 describes this generational pattern of instruction as Solomon teaches his son the same lessons he learned from his father, David: "When I was a son with my father, tender, the only one in the sight of my mother, he taught me and said to me, 'Let your heart hold fast my words; keep my commandments, and live'" (vv. 3-4). Solomon passes on three instructions for a future father who seeks to make multiple generations of disciples: Find wisdom, choose the right path, and keep a good heart. These three words of wisdom will turn boys into men.

First, find wisdom like you would find a good wife: "Get wisdom; get insight; do not forget, and do not turn away from the words of my mouth" (v. 5; see v. 7). Acquire wisdom as if paying a dowry for her hand in marriage. No cost is too great. "Do not forsake her, and she will keep you; love her, and she will guard you. . . . Prize her highly, and she will exalt you; she will honor you if you embrace her" (vv. 6, 8). "She will place on your head a graceful garland; she will bestow on you a beautiful crown" (v. 9). For a son to become a godly father, he must first make Lady Wisdom his wife.

Second, he must choose the right path by walking in the way of wisdom (vv. 10-13, 18) and avoiding the path of the wicked (vv. 14-17, 19). The decisions your child makes today will determine his destination tomorrow.

Finally, your child must keep a good heart: "My son, be attentive to my words; incline your ear to my sayings. Let them not escape from your sight; keep them within your heart. . . . Keep your heart with all vigilance, for from it flow the springs of life" (Prov. 4:20-21, 23). Each generation must pass on these truths to the generations that follow.

My wife and I recently prepared a living trust to be activated in the unfortunate case of our demise. It seemed morbid to even contemplate our death, yet we wisely recognized our mortality as we sought to leave a lasting legacy. The other day, when my oldest was hiding from his brothers, I jokingly told my second son, "You are now the eldest. You will receive all the fruits of my inheritance." Then I told my third son, "And you are the next in line." They were both extremely excited about moving up in the pecking order and disappointed that I was only joking. It made me realize, however, that my children will inherit whatever I leave them. "How much better to get wisdom than gold! To get understanding is to be chosen rather than silver" (16:16). Dads, consider today what you will pass on to your children. You might pass on your name, your wealth, or your home, but will you also pass on a lasting spiritual legacy? Begin planning for it today.

PRAYER: *Dear Heavenly Father, Cultivate in me a life of godliness so that I may leave a spiritual legacy for my children. More than property or wealth, I desire to give them what is most important. Help me to do this not just at my death, but even more so throughout my life. Then may they also pass down this legacy through many generations. In your Son's name, Amen.*

---------------□---------------

Write down one way you will apply today's Proverb:

35

SELF-CONTROL

A man without self-control
is like a city broken into and left without walls.
- PROVERBS 25:28

In the 1970s, Stanford psychologists conducted the now-famous "Marshmallow Test." They handed each child a marshmallow and instructed them, "You can eat this marshmallow whenever you want, but if you wait fifteen minutes without eating it we'll give you another one." When the researchers left the room, some of the children gobbled up their marshmallow immediately while others exercised self-control (though under visible duress). The researchers then tracked the progress of these children over the next several decades and found that the second group—the ones who waited—far excelled the first in life skills: They achieved higher grades, maintained better physical health, and were more likely to be happy in life. The driving factor in their success was self-control. Long before Stanford, however, Paul cited self-control as a qualification for spiritual leadership (Titus 1:8) and godly maturity (2:2, 5). He also gave only one instruction for training young men: "Urge the younger men to be self-controlled" (Titus 2:6).

Dads, do not be ruled by unruly heart desires. Learn to control your temper and your tongue, your ambition and your avarice, the lust of the eyes, the lust of the flesh, and the pride of life (1 John 2:16). When your heart worships any other god, you will live your life in subjection to that god: "A man without self-control is like a city broken into and left without walls" (Prov. 25:28)—unprotected from predators and enemies. Without self-control, you cannot lead your family well. For self-control undergirds godly character and establishes a well-ordered life. Many men are ineffective in the church and in the home because they are enslaved to other gods. As D. L. Moody said, "The world has yet to see what God can do with one man totally sold out to him."

Suppose you live on impulse, however, dominated by one idolatrous desire after the next. How do you cultivate self-control? First, remember Paul's instruction to fill your heart with the glories of the gospel. Jesus paid the price for sin, so that you could die to self: "For the grace of God has appeared, bringing salvation for all people, training us to renounce ungodliness and worldly passions, and to live self-controlled, upright, and godly lives in the present age" (2:11-12). The gospel trains you to say, "No," to sin and, "Yes," to Christ. Second, believe that change can happen, for Paul would not exhort you to do the impossible. The fruit of self-control in a believer's life will surely grow in the soil of the gospel (Gal. 5:22-23). Third, seek help and encouragement from older men (see Titus 2:7-8). Find solidarity in the brotherhood of Christ and look for faithful examples to follow. If your walls are broken down, find a godly man to help you rebuild.

Then dads, teach your children self-control. I often ask my boys: "*What is patience*?" They answer automatically, "To wait for something good." Yet when I ask them, "*Would you rather have $100 now or $25,000 ten years from now?*" they always choose the $100 now. Patience is easy to learn in theory, but hard to practice in reality (especially for children). On long road trips, they frequently ask: "Are we there yet?" and they become giddy with excitement the moment Christmas presents appear beneath the tree. Dads, teach your children self-control by using delayed gratification. Challenge them to save up money for a toy they really want or to hold off dessert until they finish eating vegetables. Teach them to wait for what is good.

Also train your children by modeling patience in the way you speak to them. Instead of reacting rashly, "the heart of the righteous ponders how to answer" (Prov. 15:28a). Think first before you speak, for "whoever keeps his mouth and his tongue keeps himself out of trouble" (21:23). Imagine you are the king of a medieval castle. If a nobleman, a knight, or a traveling minstrel walk into your castle, you have the right to speak as royalty. If you are merely the king's herald, however, you must await the king's decree. Your speech reflects who reigns as sovereign in your life. If you are living for the kingdom of self, you will quickly speak your mind. Yet if you are living for the kingdom of God, you will pause and reflect: "What speech would best represent my King? How would he want me to address my fellow subjects? What kind of communication would honor my spouse? How should I speak to my children even when they push my buttons?" The kingly authority in your life determines the nature of your speech, for the war of words is a war of sovereignty—a war of worship in your heart. So are you the king or simply a herald of the King?

Finally dads, teach your children how to wait on God. My son once bemoaned how he felt like Abraham and my wife took the bait, asking, "Why's that?"

He then dramatically replied, "Because I've had to wait so long for you to keep your promise."

My wife wisely responded, "Yes, but remember how God kept his promise to Abraham."

To which my son countered with rock-solid theology: "That's true, mommy, but you're not God."

Dads, always remember that you're not God. You only have the authority to speak when you speak on God's behalf. Therefore, direct your children to "wait for the LORD, and he will deliver [them]" (Prov. 20:22b). Remind them of their heavenly Father who acts for them in love: "He who did not spare his own Son but gave him up for us all, how will he not also with him graciously give us all things?" (Rom. 8:32). You are the Lord's representative and not his replacement.

PRAYER: *Dear Heavenly Father, Teach me to be self-controlled in my speech and in my actions as the spiritual leader in the home. Grant me wisdom to train my children in patience and self-control. Then shape their hearts to seek first your kingdom and not their own desires. In your Son's name, Amen.*

-------------□-------------

Write down one way you will apply today's Proverb:

—36—

FORGIVENESS

Whoever conceals his transgressions will not prosper,
but he who confesses and forsakes them will obtain mercy.
- PROVERBS 28:13

The other day I was lacking the minimum energy required just to be a parent and I snapped at one of my sons in sinful anger: "Quit being stupid!" I instantly regretted my words. He was simply being silly, but I had used that insult (forbidden in our home) to make him stop talking. My boys all laughed, thinking it funny to hear a forbidden word (especially from daddy), but I knew it was wrong. I failed to say anything at the time, but it bothered me all night long. So I went back to my son after he was already in bed and apologized: "Son, I'm sorry I spoke to you in that way. It was wrong and hurtful and I should not have said it. Will you forgive me?" I did not use my exhaustion as an excuse or cite his silliness as a trigger. He may have pushed my buttons, but they were still my buttons. So I honestly confessed my sin and sought forgiveness. Then both my son and my God forgave me and I slept with a clear conscience that night.

Dads, learning to seek your children's forgiveness is not a sign of weakness. Instead, it takes strength to humbly admit when you are wrong. Teach your children that you are also a sinner in need of grace and model for them genuine repentance. You cannot expect them to forgive and be forgiven unless you show them how it's done.

Second, instruct your children how to seek forgiveness well. Do not settle for perfunctory platitudes: "Say sorry to your brother." "*Sorry, brother.*" Instead, guide them through a proper confession: "Son, look your brother in the eye. Tell him why you are sorry and admit your wrong specifically. Don't make excuses for your actions, but take full responsibility. Then ask your brother to forgive you and accept the consequences. Okay now, everybody hug." Children tend to move on quickly, but watch for passive-aggressive behavior which reveals an unforgiving spirit. Lay a solid foundation now because the future will hold more difficult tests than sibling rivalry.

Finally, instruct your children how to forgive when they are sinned against. Forgiven sinners forgive sinners because they know the meaning of grace (e.g., Matt. 18:21-35). As Paul writes,

> Put on then, as God's chosen ones, holy and beloved, compassionate hearts, kindness, humility, meekness, and patience, bearing with one another and, if one has a complaint against another, forgiving each other; as the Lord has forgiven you, so you also must forgive. And above all these put on love, which binds everything together in perfect harmony (Col. 3:12-14).

Dads, show your children the gospel foundation of forgiveness. Our heavenly Father forgave our massive debt by sending his Son to die in our place. Though we had no credit with God, Christ's payment wiped our debit clean. How then can we cling to a grudge or fondle bitterness when we truly grasp forgiveness? Any failure to forgive means we do not fully understand either the depth of our sin or the greatness of our Savior. Every time your children are wronged, you have the blessed opportunity to rejoice in the gospel as you lead them in forgiveness.

Teach your children that forgiveness makes three promises: "I will no longer dwell on this issue in my mind, I will never again bring it up against you, and I will not gossip about it with others." Your children may be tempted to hold grudges, stew over past wrongs, or fling accusations: "You're doing it again. Remember last time?" They may be tempted to gossip or slander against the one who wronged them. So train them that all such behavior will break their promise to forgive as God in Christ forgave them (Eph. 4:32). Although God still knows their sin, he never holds it against them once that sin is pardoned (Rom. 8:1). He does not shame them before others or stew over past wrongs. "For as high as the heavens are above the earth, so great is his steadfast love toward those who fear him; as far as the east is from the west, so far does he remove our transgressions from us.

As a father shows compassion to his children, so the LORD shows compassion to those who fear him" (Ps. 103:11-13; see Prov. 28:13).

PRAYER: *Dear Heavenly Father, Thank you for your grace in forgiving my sin at the cross. Teach me to forgive my children when they disobey or disrespect me. Then help me set their hearts on a gospel foundation, so they will humbly seek forgiveness from those they have wronged and mercifully forgive those who have wronged them. In your Son's name, Amen.*

--------------□--------------

Write down one way you will apply today's Proverb:

—37—

COMFORT IN TRIALS

Whoever gives thought to the word will discover good,
and blessed is he who trusts in the LORD.

- PROVERBS 16:20

My sons were gravely confined to suits during their uncle's wedding. So right after the family pictures, they ripped off their pink bow ties and began shooting them in the air like slingshots. It was a time of raucous celebration —not over the wedding, but over their glorious freedom. That's how I picture Lazarus when he rose from the dead and threw off his graveclothes (John 11:44). That is the joy we too should have in God's deliverance (Prov. 29:2a). Even harder, however, is to maintain that joy in the midst of trials (Jas. 1:2). For the way of escape often runs through the difficulty, not around it (1 Cor. 10:13). True faith faces all of life.

Dads, speak honestly to your children about life's afflictions. It is normal to hurt and necessary to grieve: "God, those words really hurt me. I feel angry all the time. I'm too proud to ask for help." Practice the psalmist's candor: "Lord, I cannot stop my tears or push back the stubborn darkness. My enemies taunt me to doubt your presence and I long for the past when I worshipped you freely. Why are you cast down, O my soul, and why are you in turmoil within me?" (Ps. 42:3-5a). Prayer is messy, even impolite, like a child bursting through the door with a skinned-up knee. Yet a loving father will never turn away his hurting child: "Walk back through that door and try it again." Instead, he holds her close and comforts her with gentle embrace. So also, your heavenly Father hears your raw complaints, knowing they are not the finished product of your heart (Prov. 13:12a; 18:14). Your God accepts groaning as part of life in a fallen world (Rom. 8:22), yet also part of his sovereign plan (v. 28a). Are you angry or grieving a loss? Then run to the Lord in prayer. Pour out your messy heart to him and seek his refuge, for "blessed is he who trusts in the LORD" (Prov. 16:20b). "When the righteous cry for help, the LORD hears and delivers them out of all their troubles. The LORD is near to the brokenhearted and saves the crushed in spirit" (Ps. 34:17-18). Christ calls to you in the midst of your pain, just as he called forth Lazarus (John 11:43).

Dads, model emotions appropriate to each situation. Do not sing "songs to a heavy heart" (Prov. 25:20), but "weep with those who weep" (Rom. 12:15b) as Jesus wept at the tomb of Lazarus (John 11:35). Help your children grieve their losses while trusting God's purpose in the pain.

"*Is God sovereign*?" The Christian answers, "Yes!" (Lam. 3:37-38).

"*Did God prevent the trial*?" Often, the answer is, "No" (e.g., Job 1-2).

"*Then what do you think a good God is doing in the midst of your trial*?" (Gen. 50:20).

Dads, teach your children that sin ushered sorrow into the world and destroyed the paradise that once had been. Exhort them to long for heaven—a better place where life will never end in loss (Rev. 21:4). Help them find joy even in the midst of suffering, for "a joyful heart is good medicine" (Prov. 17:22a; 15:13a). Then if their heart is good, they can rejoice in the midst of any trial. Even in the throes of grief, lead them to the Shepherd who carries them gently (Ps. 28:9; Isa. 40:11). Comfort is knowing the presence of God in the presence of suffering—his strength despite their weakness (2 Cor. 12:9-10).

Dads, teach your children to receive God's comfort through his Word and warn them also against false comforts described in Proverbs: the lure of wine and women, wealth and wicked men. Many cope with loss through alcohol or illicit drugs, gluttony or hording, the rush of adrenaline or digital distraction. Wherever you turn in the face of suffering is the god you claim will save. Yet Paul declares, "Blessed be the God and Father of our Lord Jesus Christ, the Father of mercies and God of all comfort, who comforts us in all our affliction" (2 Cor. 1:3-4a). Dads, do you trust the Lord even when life hurts? Do you know the God of all comfort who designs your suffering to lead you into worship? Confident trust means longing fervently for heaven while living passionately for God on earth. So even in grief, "give thanks in all circumstances" (1 Thess. 5:18a) and perceive the evidences of God's grace. Do not wait until suffering ends, but rejoice in the midst of trials (Jas. 1:2). Do not despair, but entrust yourself to God's greater purpose—his eternal plan. God's redemptive story never ignores your pain, but rather fills it with meaning. He brings beauty out of ashes (Isa. 61:3) and "has made everything for its purpose, even the wicked for the day of trouble" (Prov. 16:4). God uses even the sin of others and the suffering we experience to bring about his good purposes.

Finally dads, teach your children the good news of the cross on which your Savior died. On that cursed tree of death (Gal. 3:13), God sent his Son to "swallow up death forever" (Isa. 25:8; Rev. 20:14) and to "destroy the one who has the power of death" (Heb. 2:14-15). Christ died so that you should not and rose again to claim his victory. So although this fallen world still echoes death, you know how the story ends. The One who weeps with you in suffering is not content with life as is. His death was a cry (John 19:30) and his resurrection a promise (1 Pet. 1:3). So look to Jesus, "[the] man of sorrows acquainted with grief" (Isa. 53:3) who will one day wipe away every tear (Rev. 7:17; 21:4). "In this world you will have tribulation. But take heart; [Jesus] has overcome the world" (John 16:33b). "A crushed spirit who can bear" (Prov. 18:14b)? Only Christ!

PRAYER: *Dear Heavenly Father, Thank you for your gracious comfort in my affliction. I can truly count it all joy in the midst of trials when I am trusting in your sovereign plan. Help me to shepherd my children through any grief and loss they face in life and teach us always to fix our eyes on our glorious eternity with you. In your Son's name, Amen.*

-------------□-------------

Write down one way you will apply today's Proverb:

38

LEGALISM

To do righteousness and justice
is more acceptable to the LORD than sacrifice.
- PROVERBS 21:3

Dads, your children have a foolish, self-centered plan to rebel against God (Ps. 14:1). So make it your goal to not merely change behavior, but to transform hearts. Grace tells them, "Jesus is your Savior," but the law shows them why they need one. One of my sons never needed convincing that he was sinful: "Daddy, it's so hard to be good!" Another son, however, tended to be more pharisaical: "God, I thank you that I am not like other men, extortioners, unjust, adulterers, or even like this tax collector" (Luke 18:11). Such legalistic tendencies are more the norm as children struggle to obey God's law (Deut. 6:6-9).

God's law, however, is the forerunner of the gospel (e.g., Matt. 3:2). It may expose your child's sin, but it cannot save. It may reveal his need for a Savior, but it cannot change his heart. For example, it is good to teach your child: "Lying lips are an abomination to the LORD, but those who act faithfully are his delight" (Prov. 12:22). The law says, "Don't tell lies." Yet the law does not exist to make your child an honest Pharisee. Instead, you faithfully reinforce God's law until your child realizes he can't obey it. The law reveals his failure and that failure will lead to Jesus. Dads, train your child to recognize lying as a sin according to God's law. His conscience may already be at work (Rom. 2:14-15), yet God's law brings conviction. As Paul writes, "If it had not been for the law, I would not have known sin" (7:7b). The law exposes your child's guilt and guilt will lead him to trust in Jesus. Only Christ can give him a brand new heart which desires to keep God's law (Ezek. 36:26-27). This good news transforms obedience from duty to delight.

Dads, also watch out for two perversions of the gospel: lawlessness and legalism. The lawless father lets his child do whatever she wants. This child thinks herself inherently righteous because she never knows her sin. She does not realize she needs a Savior because she views herself as god. She misses out on Jesus because she does not know the law.

The legalistic father, however, controls everything his child does. This child never learns that he is loved and thinks he has to save himself. He futilely attempts to earn his father's favor and applies the same works-salvation to his relationship with God. He too misses out on Jesus because he does not know God's grace (Prov. 21:3). Legalism cares more about behavior than the heart.

Dads, do not lean too far to either lawlessness or legalism. Instead, focus on the full-orbed gospel, for you train the heart by the way you motivate obedience. Suppose one child angrily hits another. You might seek to control him with fear or threats: "Hit your sister again and I'll hit you!"

You might offer rewards: "If you both behave for the rest of the meal, we'll all have ice cream."

Sometimes you tempt with comfort or pleasure: "Be nice to your sister and she'll leave you alone."

At other times, you resort to shame: "You're such a terrible child. You never listen. Why can't you be more like the pastor's kids?"

You might even motivate your child's heart with guilt: "What you did was very, very bad. You need to behave yourself."

Dads, pay attention! Any time you discipline your child, you are teaching her what to love. You are training his heart's desire by what you use for motivation. So instead of threats and rewards and shame, offer your child Jesus: "Son, that was wrong to hit your sister. Violence is a sin that so angered the holy God that he poured out his wrath on Jesus at the cross. But son, God loves you and wants to enjoy a relationship with you. He wants to forgive your sin and heal that broken relationship. Will you make things right with Jesus and embrace him as your friend? He can forgive your sinful anger, then teach you how to love your sister rightly."

Dads, beware of both lawlessness and legalism, for discipline must always be redemptive. Instead of gauging, "Is my child behaving correctly," consider, "Has my child grown closer to Jesus?" You will never reach your child's heart with lecture: "*Why did you hit your sister*?" "I don't know." Instead, ask questions to reach his heart: "What emotions were you feeling when you hit your sister?" "What did she do to spark your anger?" "How else could you have responded?" "Help me understand how your response seemed to make things better." "How do you think your anger reflected trust or lack of trust in God's ability to care for you?" By gently probing his heart, you might learn your son responded angrily when his sister took the last slice of pizza. He was controlled by a selfish appetite for the pleasure of pizza, desiring comfort food over his sister's well-being.

Then as you pull your son aside, you do not simply teach him that hitting is wrong, but that selfishness itself is wrong: "Son, God made our bodies to enjoy delicious food, yet those desires become idolatrous when we make them our demands. Those demands then influence us to judge and punish people we love. Yet God promises to forgive your selfishness if you confess your sin right now (Prov. 28:13)." As you lead your son in confession, exhort him to ask forgiveness both for his angry behavior and for his selfish motives. Every time your child sins, God graciously gives you another opportunity to address not simply behavior, but also his sinful heart desires. Redemptive discipline shows your child that he is a sinner in desperate need of a Savior.

PRAYER: *Dear Heavenly Father, Forgive me for my own self-righteousness as a father and my idolatrous desire for well-behaved children. Help me to recognize my own sin that tempts me to be either a lawless or a legalistic parent. Show me how to lovingly instruct my children according to your law, but also to see every failure as a chance to point them to the good news of Jesus. In your Son's name, Amen.*

-------------□-------------

Write down one way you will apply today's Proverb:

39

GOOD NEWS

By steadfast love and faithfulness iniquity is atoned for,
and by the fear of the LORD one turns away from evil.
- PROVERBS 16:6

My toddler once decided it would be fun to leap into the pool without daddy there to catch him. My wife (who cannot swim herself) saw this happen as if in slow motion and jumped fully-clothed into the pool to save him. So also, dads, be ready to rescue your foolish children with the gospel, for without Christ they will never stay spiritually afloat. Learn how to swim yourself by daily meditating on Christ's finished work. Then keep proclaiming the gospel as a drowning man to drowning children.

I love the account in C. S. Lewis's, *The Lion, the Witch, and the Wardrobe* of Edmund's redemption. Edmund betrays his three siblings to the White Witch who plans to murder them all. Although he is later rescued by the forces of good, the evil Witch declares that Edmund still belongs to her: "Every traitor belongs to me as my lawful prey and . . . for every treachery I have a right to a kill." The Witch is about to take his life, until Aslan—the Jesus figure in the story, offers his own life in Edmund's place. That night, surrounded by the forces of evil, Aslan willingly succumbs to death while the Witch rejoices. Only when Aslan rises from the dead does he explain to his loyal followers

> that though the Witch knew the Deep Magic, there is a magic deeper still which she did not know. Her knowledge goes back only to the dawn of time. But if she could have looked a little further back, into the stillness and the darkness before Time dawned, she would have read there a different incantation.

> She would have known that when a willing victim who had committed no treachery was killed in a traitor's stead, the Table would crack and Death itself would start working backwards.

After reading this story with my boys, I jokingly asked them, "Which of you would sell out his brothers for another piece of Turkish delight?" The sad truth, however, is that we are all like Edmund. We are all traitors, liars, thieves, and murderers deserving God's judgment and condemned by his law. Yet Scripture tells the deeper magic of a spotless Savior who sacrificed his own life for ours and rose from the dead to conquer sin and death. Because of Jesus, we are forgiven of sin and empowered to flee temptation. We discover greater joy in Christ than in the worthless idols of this world, so let us run to Jesus and find his comfort at the cross.

The gospel begins with God—his attributes and his marvelous works. He is Creator of all (Prov. 3:19; 22:2), omniscient and omnipresent (15:3), sovereign (16:9, 33), just (17:15), gracious (28:13), and worthy of worship (Rev. 4:11).

By contrast, man is sinful (Prov. 20:9; Rom. 3:10-12) and foolish from birth (Prov. 22:15). He is blinded to sin (12:15a) and does not respond to the good news proclaimed: "Fools despise wisdom and instruction" (1:7b; 14:9). He cannot save himself by good works (21:3, 27; Eph. 2:8-9) and therefore deserves God's judgment (Prov. 6:33; 19:29; see Heb. 9:27).

Yet thankfully, Jesus took the penalty for sin upon himself (2 Cor. 5:21) and forgave our folly (Isa. 53:5): "By steadfast love and faithfulness iniquity is atoned for, and by the fear of the LORD one turns away from evil" (Prov. 16:6). Only those who turn to Christ can be forgiven and only those who admit their sin can be made righteous (28:13), for God sacrificed his beloved Son that we might have eternal life (John 3:16; Rom. 5:8). This is the greatest love that a man "lay down his life for his friends" (Prov. 15:13). In Christ, we learn that righteousness is better than riches because it leads us to eternal life (11:4). Christ's death made reconciliation between us and God and brought us once more into relationship with the Father (1 Pet. 3:18).

But that's not all! For Jesus rose from the dead after three days in the tomb, declaring victory over sin and death. We therefore ground our living hope in the resurrection victory of Christ (1:3). How can we do anything else but praise his name! So flee to safety at the cross of Christ. Rejoice in his forgiveness and delight in his redemption. Thank him for his life-preserving, sin-mortifying strength. The power of the cross is the power of the gospel (Rom. 1:16; 6:23).

Dads, if you have unbelieving children, urge them to follow Christ as Lord (10:9): "Be not wise in your own eyes; fear the LORD, and turn away from evil" (Prov. 3:7). And if you have believing children, exhort them to continue in the faith: "Keep your heart with all vigilance, for from it flow the springs of life" (4:23). Centering their worship on the fear of the Lord (1:7a) will result in everlasting life (14:27).

PRAYER: *Dear Heavenly Father, I am a sinful man, unable to be a good father by any merit of my own. I fail in a thousand ways and deserve a thousand punishments, yet you are gracious, O Lord. Out of love, you sent your Son to take my place. He died for me and forgave my sin. Thank you for your saving grace and for the grace to continue growing as a father. Teach me always to run to you both in times of need and times of celebration. In your Son's name, Amen.*

--------------□--------------

Write down one way you will apply today's Proverb:

40

THE FEAR OF THE LORD

In the fear of the LORD one has strong confidence,
and his children will have a refuge.
The fear of the LORD is a fountain of life,
that one may turn away from the snares of death.
- PROVERBS 14:26-27

The other day I was installing a crystal chandelier in the nursery when I happened to read comments on the company website by other brave souls who had tried and failed before me. Most of those comments were posted by husbands griping about all the tiny little pieces and how the finely printed instructions were of less value than toilet paper. A rare few comments came from wives gushing over how thrilled they were that their husbands had finally installed the chandelier and how it brightened up their home.

I realize it is now my turn to try my hand at this Herculean task and I reach the step of connecting the wires. Since I always get nervous working with electricity, I dutifully ran downstairs to the circuit breaker and shut off the power before going back up to connect the wires. I then went down to turn the power back on, but returned to find the light in the chandelier still off. The other lights in the room were working, so maybe the bulb was bad. I switched out the bulb, but it wasn't the bulb. I then considered that maybe I had crossed the wires, so I ran down to turn off the circuit breaker again before running back up to re-connect the wires. I went back down to turn the power on then ran back up, but the light was still not working. My electrical expertise had reached its limit, so I now had no idea what to do. I was frustrated and about to give up. Maybe I'd add my own complaints to the company website. I even considered re-connecting the wires like they were at first (as if that would do any good). And then it hit me! The light switch was off. There was no power because the light switch in room was off.

Dads, this is a picture of parenting without God's Holy Spirit. Some of you are working really hard to understand the wisdom of God's Word. You might attend church every Sunday and listen to every sermon. You ask Christian friends or family members for advice. If you are really courageous, you might have read a book on biblical parenting (like this one!). You are constantly connecting and re-connecting the wires, turning the circuit breaker on and off as you run up and down the stairs. You are frustrated because you feel you've tried everything. Yet all the time, the light switch is off. You have no power from God's Holy Spirit to explain to you his Word (1 Cor. 2:11-14). You might understand the words intellectually, but spiritually you have no clue how wisdom illuminates your life. The light will never go on without God's Holy Spirit. Yet Lady Wisdom cries aloud for you to listen: "How long, O simple ones, will you love being simple? How long will scoffers delight in their scoffing and fools hate knowledge? If you turn at my reproof, behold, I will pour out my spirit to you; I will make my words known to you" (Prov. 1:22-23).

Dads, you cannot raise your children "in the discipline and instruction of the Lord" (Eph. 6:4b) unless you know the Lord. You cannot be filled with God's Word unless you are filled with God's Holy Spirit (Col. 3:16). You cannot communicate to your children the good news of Jesus Christ unless Jesus is first your Lord and Savior (Rom. 10:13-15). Thus we conclude Day 40 with the same truth from Day 1: "In the fear of the LORD one has strong confidence, and his children will have a refuge. The fear of the LORD is a fountain of life, that one may turn away from the snares of death" (Prov. 14:26-27). The fear of the Lord requires both reverent obedience and worshipful joy. So obey the Lord with reverence, knowing that he alone holds the key to life and death. Then worship the Lord with joy, knowing that he alone is your strength and the refuge for your children. Dads, "serve the LORD with fear, and rejoice with trembling" (Ps. 2:11), so that your children will know him and fear him also.

PRAYER: *Dear Heavenly Father, Teach me to live my life in worshipful joy and reverent obedience. Allow my love for you to become a refuge for my children. Show me how to fear you alone and to lead my children in the path of life. In your Son's name, Amen.*

-------------□-------------

Write down one way you will apply today's Proverb:

Made in the USA
Monee, IL
04 December 2025

37313747R00073